# PYTHON

## FOR DATA ANALYST

A Comprehensive Guide
to Master Python for
Data Analyst

**David Mark**

**ISBN: 979-8-3216-6462-9**

# Table of Contents

# Introduction to Python

## Writing and Running Your First Python Program

Python is an interpreted language, which means that you can write and execute your code without compiling it. You can run Python code in different ways, such as using an interactive shell, a script file, or an integrated development environment (IDE).

To write and run your first Python program, follow these steps:

- Open a text editor of your choice and create a new file named `hello.py`.
- Type the following code in the file:

```
# This is a comment. Comments start with a # symbol and are
ignored by Python.
print("Hello, world!") # This is a print function. It
displays a message to the console.
```

- Save the file and run it using one of the following methods:
- If you have Python installed on your computer, open a terminal or command prompt and navigate to the folder where you saved the file. Then type `python hello.py` and press enter.
- If you don't have Python installed on your computer, you can use an online Python interpreter, such as Repl.it. Copy and paste the code into the editor and click the run button.
- You should see the message `Hello, world!` displayed on the console.

## Indentation and Whitespace

Unlike many other programming languages, Python uses indentation and whitespace to indicate the structure and hierarchy of the code. This means that the amount of space before a line of code determines its level of indentation, and the indentation level of a block of code determines its scope.

For example, consider the following code:

```
if x > 10: # This is an if statement. It checks a condition
and executes a block of code if it is true.
    print("x is greater than 10") # This line is indented by
four spaces. It belongs to the if block.
    if x > 20: # This is a nested if statement. It checks
another condition within the if block.
        print("x is also greater than 20") # This line is
indented by eight spaces. It belongs to the nested if block.
else: # This is an else statement. It executes a block of
code if the condition of the if statement is false.
    print("x is not greater than 10") # This line is indented
by four spaces. It belongs to the else block.
```

In this code, the indentation levels indicate which lines of code belong to which blocks. The if and else statements have the same indentation level, which means they are at the same level of hierarchy. The nested if statement and its print function have a higher indentation level, which means they are within the scope of the outer if statement. The indentation also makes the code more readable and organized.

Python does not have a fixed rule for the number of spaces to use for indentation, but it is recommended to use four spaces for each level. You should also be consistent and use the same amount of spaces throughout your code. Mixing spaces and tabs for indentation can cause errors and confusion.

# Variables and Data Types in Python

A variable is a name that refers to a value stored in the memory. You can use variables to store and manipulate data in your program. To create a variable in Python, you simply assign a value to a name using the = operator. For example:

```
name = "Alice" # This creates a variable named name and
assigns it the value "Alice".
age = 25 # This creates a variable named age and assigns it
the value 25.
```

You can use any name for your variables, as long as they follow these rules:

- They must start with a letter or an underscore (_), but not a number or a symbol.

- They can contain letters, numbers, and underscores, but not spaces or other symbols.
- They must not be a reserved word in Python, such as `if`, `else`, `print`, etc.

Python is a dynamically typed language, which means that you do not have to specify the type of the variable when you create it. Python automatically infers the type of the variable based on the value assigned to it. You can check the type of a variable using the `type()` function. For example:

```
type(name) # This returns <class 'str'>, which means name is
a string.
type(age) # This returns <class 'int'>, which means age is an
integer.
```

Python has several built-in data types, such as:

- **Integers**: These are whole numbers, such as `1`, `0`, `-5`, etc. They have no decimal point or fractional part. You can use them for counting, arithmetic, and indexing.
- **Floats**: These are numbers with a decimal point or a fractional part, such as `3.14`, `0.5`, `-2.7`, etc. You can use them for measurements, calculations, and scientific notation.
- Strings: These are sequences of characters, such as "Hello", "Python", "42", etc. You can use them for text, labels, and symbols. You can create a string by enclosing characters in single (' ') or double (" ") quotes.
- Lists: These are ordered collections of values, such as [1, 2, 3], ["a", "b", "c"], [True, False, None], etc. You can use them to store and manipulate multiple values of the same or different types. You can create a list by enclosing values in square brackets ([ ]).
- Dictionaries: These are unordered collections of key-value pairs, such as {"name": "Alice", "age": 25, "gender": "female"}, {"x": 1, "y": 2, "z": 3}, {"a": True, "b": False, "c": None}, etc. You can use them to store and access values by their keys. You can create a dictionary by enclosing key-value pairs in curly braces ({ }).

There are other data types in Python, such as tuples, sets, booleans, and None.

# Operators

An operator is a symbol that performs a specific operation on one or more values. Python supports various types of operators, such as:

**Arithmetic operators**: These are used to perform mathematical operations on numeric values, such as addition (+), subtraction (-), multiplication (*), division (/), modulus (%), exponentiation (**), and floor division (//). For example:

```
x = 10
y = 3
print(x + y) # This prints 13, the result of adding x and y.
print(x - y) # This prints 7, the result of subtracting y
from x.
print(x * y) # This prints 30, the result of multiplying x
and y.
print(x / y) # This prints 3.3333333333333335, the result of
dividing x by y.
print(x % y) # This prints 1, the remainder of dividing x by
y.
print(x ** y) # This prints 1000, the result of raising x to
the power of y.
print(x // y) # This prints 3, the result of dividing x by y
and rounding down to the nearest integer.
```

**Assignment operators**: These are used to assign values to variables, such as equal (=), plus equal (+=), minus equal (-=), multiply equal (*=), divide equal (/=), modulus equal (%=), exponent equal (**=), and floor divide equal (//=). For example:

```
x = 10 # This assigns 10 to x.
x += 5 # This is equivalent to x = x + 5. It adds 5 to x and
assigns the result to x.
x -= 5 # This is equivalent to x = x - 5. It subtracts 5 from
x and assigns the result to x.
x *= 5 # This is equivalent to x = x * 5. It multiplies x by
5 and assigns the result to x.
x /= 5 # This is equivalent to x = x / 5. It divides x by 5
and assigns the result to x.
x %= 5 # This is equivalent to x = x % 5. It calculates the
remainder of dividing x by 5 and assigns the result to x.
x **= 5 # This is equivalent to x = x ** 5. It raises x to
the power of 5 and assigns the result to x.
x //= 5 # This is equivalent to x = x // 5. It divides x by 5
```

```
and rounds down to the nearest integer and assigns the result
to x.
```

# Conditional Statements and Loops

Conditional statements and loops are used to control the flow of a Python program, depending on certain conditions or iterations. They allow you to execute different blocks of code based on different situations or repeat the same block of code multiple times.

## Conditional Statements

A conditional statement is a statement that checks a condition and executes a block of code if the condition is true, or another block of code if the condition is false. The most common conditional statement in Python is the `if-else` statement, which has the following syntax:

```
if condition:
    # This block of code is executed if the condition is
true.
else:
    # This block of code is executed if the condition is
false.
```

The `condition` can be any expression that evaluates to a boolean value (`True` or `False`). The `if` and `else` keywords are followed by a colon (`:`), and the blocks of code are indented by four spaces. For example:

```
x = 10
if x > 0:
    print("x is positive")
else:
    print("x is negative or zero")
```

This code checks if the value of `x` is greater than zero, and prints a message accordingly. You can also use the `elif` keyword to add more conditions and blocks of code, such as:

```
x = 10
if x > 0:
    print("x is positive")
elif x < 0:
    print("x is negative")
else:
```

```
    print("x is zero")
```

This code checks if the value of `x` is positive, negative, or zero, and prints a message accordingly. You can have as many `elif` clauses as you want, but only one `else` clause at the end. The `else` clause is optional, and you can omit it if you don't need it.

## Loops

A loop is a statement that repeats a block of code until a certain condition is met or for a certain number of times. The most common loops in Python are the `for` loop and the `while` loop, which have the following syntax:

```
for variable in iterable:
    # This block of code is executed for each element in the
iterable.

while condition:
    # This block of code is executed while the condition is
true.
```

The `for` loop iterates over an iterable object, such as a list, a string, or a range, and assigns each element to a variable. The `while` loop executes a block of code as long as a condition is true. The `for` and `while` keywords are followed by a colon (`:`), and the blocks of code are indented by four spaces. For example:

```
for i in range(5):
    print(i)
```

This code prints the numbers from 0 to 4, using the `range()` function to create an iterable object of five elements.

```
n = 1
while n < 10:
    print(n)
    n = n * 2
```

This code prints the powers of 2 that are less than 10, using a variable `n` to store the current value and update it in each iteration.

You can use the `break` statement to exit a loop prematurely, or the `continue` statement to skip the current iteration and move to the next one.

For example:

```
for i in range(10):
    if i == 5:
        break # This stops the loop when i is 5.
    print(i)
```

This code prints the numbers from 0 to 4, and then stops the loop when `i` is 5.

```
for i in range(10):
    if i % 2 == 0:
        continue # This skips the even numbers.
    print(i)
```

This code prints the odd numbers from 1 to 9, and skips the even numbers using the modulo operator (%) to check the remainder of dividing `i` by 2.

# Input and Output in Python

Input and output are essential for any program to interact with the user and the environment. Python provides several built-in functions and modules to perform input and output operations, such as:

**The `print()` function**: This is the most basic and common output function in Python. It displays one or more values to the console, separated by spaces, and followed by a newline character. You can use the `sep` and `end` parameters to change the separator and the ending characters, respectively. For example:

```
print("Hello, world!") # This prints "Hello, world!" to the console.
print("Hello", "world", sep=", ") # This prints "Hello, world" to the console, using a comma and a space as the separator.
print("Hello", "world", end="!") # This prints "Hello world!" to the console, using an exclamation mark as the ending character.
```

**The `input()` function**: This is the most basic and common input function in Python. It prompts the user to enter a value from the keyboard and returns it as a string. You can pass a string as an argument to the function to display a message to the user. For example:

```
name = input("What is your name? ") # This prompts the user
to enter their name and assigns it to the variable name.
print("Hello, " + name) # This prints a greeting message to
the user, using string concatenation to join the strings.
```

**The `open()` function and the `file` object**: These are used to open and manipulate files in Python. The `open()` function takes a file name and a mode as arguments and returns a file object that represents the file. The mode can be `'r'` for reading, `'w'` for writing, `'a'` for appending, or `'x'` for creating. You can also add a `'b'` to the mode to indicate binary mode, or a `'+'` to indicate updating mode. For example:

```
f = open("test.txt", "w") # This opens a file named test.txt
in write mode and assigns it to the variable f.
f.write("This is a test.") # This writes a string to the
file.
f.close() # This closes the file and saves the changes.
```

The file object has several methods and attributes to perform various operations on the file, such as `read()`, `write()`, `seek()`, `tell()`, `name`, `mode`, etc. You can also use the `with` statement to automatically close the file after the block of code is executed. For example:

```
with open("test.txt", "r") as f: # This opens a file named
test.txt in read mode and assigns it to the variable f.
    content = f.read() # This reads the entire content of the
file and assigns it to the variable content.
    print(content) # This prints the content of the file to
the console.
# The file is automatically closed after the with block is
executed.
```

**The `os` module**: This is a module that provides various functions and attributes to interact with the operating system, such as creating, deleting, renaming, and moving files and directories, getting and changing the current working directory, getting and setting environment variables, etc. You can import the module using the `import` statement and use the dot (`.`) operator to access its functions and attributes. For example:

```
import os # This imports the os module.
os.mkdir("new_folder") # This creates a new folder named
new_folder in the current working directory.
os.rename("new_folder", "old_folder") # This renames the
```

```
new_folder to old_folder.
os.rmdir("old_folder") # This deletes the old_folder.
print(os.getcwd()) # This prints the current working
directory.
print(os.listdir()) # This prints a list of files and folders
in the current working directory.
print(os.environ["PATH"]) # This prints the value of the PATH
environment variable.
```

# String Manipulation

A string is a sequence of characters, such as "Hello", "Python", "42", etc. You can create a string by enclosing characters in single (' ') or double (" ") quotes. Strings are immutable, which means that you cannot change their contents once they are created. However, you can perform various operations on strings, such as:

**String concatenation**: This is the operation of joining two or more strings together using the + operator. For example:

```
first_name = "Alice"
last_name = "Smith"
full_name = first_name + " " + last_name # This joins the
first_name, a space, and the last_name using the + operator.
print(full_name) # This prints "Alice Smith".
```

**String slicing**: This is the operation of extracting a substring from a string using the square bracket (`[ ]`) notation. You can specify the start and end indices of the substring, separated by a colon (`:`). The start index is inclusive, while the end index is exclusive. You can also specify a step size, which indicates how many characters to skip between each index. For example:

```
s = "Hello, world!"
print(s[0]) # This prints "H", the first character of the
string.
print(s[1:5]) # This prints "ello", the substring from index
1 to index 4.
print(s[7:]) # This prints "world!", the substring from index
7 to the end of the string.
print(s[:5]) # This prints "Hello", the substring from the
beginning of the string to index 4.
print(s[-1]) # This prints "!", the last character of the
string.
```

```
print(s[-6:-2]) # This prints "worl", the substring from index -6 to index -3.
print(s[::2]) # This prints "Hlo ol!", the substring with every second character of the string.
print(s[::-1]) # This prints "!dlrow ,olleH", the reversed string.
```

String slicing is useful for accessing and modifying parts of a string. You can also use it with other data types that are iterable, such as lists and tuples.

**String formatting**: This is the operation of inserting values into a string using placeholders and formatting options. You can use the `format()` method or the f-string syntax to perform string formatting. For example:

```
name = "Alice"
age = 25
print("My name is {} and I am {} years old.".format(name, age)) # This uses the format() method to insert the values of name and age into the string.
print(f"My name is {name} and I am {age} years old.") # This uses the f-string syntax to insert the values of name and age into the string.
```

String formatting is useful for creating dynamic and customized strings. You can also use various formatting options to specify the alignment, width, precision, and type of the values. For example:

```
pi = 3.14159
print("The value of pi is {:.2f}".format(pi)) # This uses the format() method to insert the value of pi into the string, with two decimal places.
print(f"The value of pi is {pi:.2f}") # This uses the f-string syntax to insert the value of pi into the string, with two decimal places.
```

**String methods**: These are built-in functions that perform various operations on strings, such as changing the case, splitting, joining, replacing, searching, etc. You can use the dot (`.`) operator to access and call these methods on a string. For example:

```
s = "Hello, world!"
print(s.upper()) # This prints "HELLO, WORLD!", the uppercase version of the string.
print(s.lower()) # This prints "hello, world!", the lowercase version of the string.
```

```
print(s.split()) # This prints ["Hello,", "world!"], a list of substrings separated by whitespace.
print(s.split(",")) # This prints ["Hello", " world!"], a list of substrings separated by a comma.
print(" ".join(["Hello", "world!"])) # This prints "Hello world!", a string joined by a space.
print(s.replace("world", "Python")) # This prints "Hello, Python!", a string with "world" replaced by "Python".
print(s.find("world")) # This prints 7, the index of the first occurrence of "world" in the string.
print(s.count("o")) # This prints 2, the number of times "o" appears in the string.
```

String methods are useful for manipulating and analyzing strings. You can also use the `help()` function or the `dir()` function to get more information about these methods. For example:

```
help(str) # This prints the documentation of the str class, which contains all the string methods and attributes.
dir(str) # This prints a list of all the string methods and attributes.
```

# Type Casting

Type casting is the process of converting one data type to another data type in Python. For example, you can convert an integer to a float, a string to a boolean, a list to a tuple, etc. Type casting can be done using built-in functions that take the original value as an argument and return the converted value. For example:

```
x = 10 # This is an integer
y = float(x) # This converts x to a float and assigns it to y
print(y) # This prints 10.0
```

Some of the most common type casting functions in Python are:

- `int()` - This converts a value to an integer. It can take a float, a string, or a boolean as an argument. If the argument is a float, it truncates the decimal part. If the argument is a string, it must represent a valid integer, otherwise it raises a `ValueError`. If the argument is a boolean, it returns 1 for `True` and 0 for `False`.
- `float()` - This converts a value to a float. It can take an integer, a string, or a boolean as an argument. If the argument is an integer, it adds a

decimal point. If the argument is a string, it must represent a valid float or an integer, otherwise it raises a `ValueError`. If the argument is a boolean, it returns 1.0 for `True` and 0.0 for `False`.

- `str()` - This converts a value to a string. It can take any data type as an argument. It returns a string representation of the value, using quotes for strings, brackets for lists and tuples, braces for sets and dictionaries, etc.
- `bool()` - This converts a value to a boolean. It can take any data type as an argument. It returns `True` for any value that is considered truthy, and `False` for any value that is considered falsy. Truthy values are non-zero numbers, non-empty strings, lists, tuples, sets, dictionaries, etc. Falsy values are zero, `None`, empty strings, lists, tuples, sets, dictionaries, etc.
- `list()` - This converts a value to a list. It can take an iterable object as an argument, such as a string, a tuple, a set, a dictionary, etc. It returns a list containing the elements of the iterable object, in the same order. If the argument is not iterable, it raises a `TypeError`.
- `tuple()` - This converts a value to a tuple. It can take an iterable object as an argument, such as a string, a list, a set, a dictionary, etc. It returns a tuple containing the elements of the iterable object, in the same order. If the argument is not iterable, it raises a `TypeError`.
- `set()` - This converts a value to a set. It can take an iterable object as an argument, such as a string, a list, a tuple, a dictionary, etc. It returns a set containing the unique elements of the iterable object, in no particular order. If the argument is not iterable, it raises a `TypeError`.
- `dict()` - This converts a value to a dictionary. It can take an iterable object as an argument, such as a list, a tuple, a set, etc. The iterable object must contain pairs of values, where the first value is the key and the second value is the value. It returns a dictionary containing the key-value pairs of the iterable object. If the argument is not iterable, or the iterable object does not contain pairs of values, it raises a `TypeError` or a `ValueError`.

Type casting is useful for changing the data type of a value to suit the needs of a program or a function. For example, you can use type casting to convert user input to the appropriate data type, to perform arithmetic operations on different data types, to compare values of different data types, etc.

# Data Structures

In this chapter, you will learn about the different types of data structures in Python, such as lists, tuples, dictionaries, sets, and deques. You will also learn how to create, modify, access, and manipulate data structures using various methods and techniques. You will also explore some advanced concepts such as nesting, hashing, aliasing, copying, and converting data structures. By the end of this chapter, you will be able to:

- Understand the basics of data structures and their properties
- Create and use lists, tuples, dictionaries, sets, and deques in Python
- Perform indexing, slicing, merging, and combining operations on data structures
- Use built-in functions and comprehensions to create and manipulate data structures
- Sort, reverse, and transform data structures using various criteria and functions
- Iterate over data structures using loops and iterators
- Test for membership and subset relations among data structures
- Avoid common pitfalls and errors when working with data structures

## List

A list is a mutable, ordered, and heterogeneous sequence of values in Python. A list can contain any type of data, such as numbers, strings, booleans, or even other lists. A list is created by enclosing the values in square brackets `[ ]`, separated by commas.

For example:

```
# A list of numbers
numbers = [1, 2, 3, 4, 5]

# A list of strings
names = ["Alice", "Bob", "Charlie"]

# A list of mixed types
```

```
mixed = [True, 3.14, "Hello", [6, 7, 8]]
```

## Indexing and Slicing Lists

To access a single element from a list, you can use the index operator `[ ]` with the index of the element inside. The index starts from 0 for the first element and goes up to the length of the list minus one for the last element. You can also use negative indices to access elements from the end of the list, starting from -1 for the last element and going down to -length for the first element.

For example:

```
# Accessing the first element
first = numbers[0] # 1

# Accessing the last element
last = names[-1] # "Charlie"

# Accessing the second element from the end
second_last = mixed[-2] # "Hello"
```

To access a range of elements from a list, you can use the slice operator `[ ]` with the start and end indices separated by a colon `:`. The slice will include the element at the start index and exclude the element at the end index. You can also omit the start or end index to indicate the beginning or the end of the list, respectively. For example:

```
# Slicing the first three elements
first_three = numbers[0:3] # [1, 2, 3]

# Slicing the last two elements
last_two = names[-2:] # ["Bob", "Charlie"]

# Slicing the middle two elements
middle_two = mixed[1:3] # [3.14, "Hello"]
```

## Mutability and Aliasing of Lists

One of the key properties of lists is that they are mutable, meaning that you can change their elements without creating a new list. You can use the assignment operator = to modify an element or a slice of a list.

For example:

```
# Modifying the first element
numbers[0] = 10
print(numbers) # [10, 2, 3, 4, 5]

# Modifying the last two elements
names[-2:] = ["David", "Eve"]
print(names) # ["Alice", "David", "Eve"]

# Modifying the middle two elements
mixed[1:3] = [False, 2.71]
print(mixed) # [True, False, 2.71, [6, 7, 8]]
```

However, this also means that you have to be careful when assigning a list to another variable, as this will create an alias, or a reference to the same list, rather than a copy. This means that any changes made to one variable will affect the other variable as well.

For example:

```
# Assigning a list to another variable
numbers_copy = numbers
print(numbers_copy) # [10, 2, 3, 4, 5]

# Modifying the original list
numbers[1] = 20
print(numbers) # [10, 20, 3, 4, 5]

# The alias is also modified
print(numbers_copy) # [10, 20, 3, 4, 5]
```

To avoid this, you can use the copy method `.copy()` or the slice operator `[ ]` with no arguments to create a shallow copy of a list, which will have the same elements but be a different object.

For example:

```
# Creating a shallow copy of a list
numbers=[10, 20, 3, 4, 5]
numbers_copy = numbers.copy()
print(numbers_copy) # [10, 20, 3, 4, 5]

# Modifying the original list
numbers[2] = 30
print(numbers) # [10, 20, 30, 4, 5]

# The copy is not modified
```

```
print(numbers_copy) # [10, 20, 3, 4, 5]
```

However, note that a shallow copy will only copy the first level of the list, and any nested lists will still be references to the same objects. To create a deep copy of a list, which will recursively copy all the elements and nested lists, you can use the copy module and its deepcopy function.

For example:

```
# Importing the copy module
import copy

# Creating a deep copy of a list
mixed_copy = copy.deepcopy(mixed)
print(mixed_copy) # [True, False, 2.71, [6, 7, 8]]

# Modifying the original list
mixed[3][0] = 9
print(mixed) # [True, False, 2.71, [9, 7, 8]]

# The copy is not modified
print(mixed_copy) # [True, False, 2.71, [6, 7, 8]]
```

## Built-in Functions and Methods for Lists

Python provides many built-in functions and methods that can be used to perform various operations on lists. Some of the most common ones are:

- `len(list)` returns the number of elements in a list
- `min(list)` returns the smallest element in a list
- `max(list)` returns the largest element in a list
- `sum(list)` returns the sum of all the elements in a list
- `sorted(list)` returns a new list with the elements sorted in ascending order
- `reversed(list)` returns a reversed iterator over the elements of a list
- `list.append(element)` adds an element to the end of a list
- `list.insert(index, element)` inserts an element at a given index in a list

- `list.remove(element)` removes the first occurrence of an element from a list
- `list.pop(index)` removes and returns the element at a given index from a list
- `list.index(element)` returns the index of the first occurrence of an element in a list
- `list.count(element)` returns the number of times an element appears in a list
- `list.extend(iterable)` adds all the elements of an iterable to the end of a list
- `list.clear()` removes all the elements from a list

For example:

```
# Using some built-in functions and methods on lists
names = ["Alice", "Eve", "David"]
mixed = [9, 2.71, False, True]
numbers = [10, 20, 30, 4, 5, 6]
print(len(numbers)) # 5
print(min(names)) # "Alice"
print(max(mixed)) # 9
print(sum(numbers)) # 69
print(sorted(names)) # ["Alice", "David", "Eve"]
print(list(reversed(mixed))) # [True,False, 2.71,9]

numbers.append(6)
print(numbers) # [10, 20, 30, 4, 5, 6]

names.insert(1, "Bob")
print(names) # ["Alice", "Bob", "Eve", "David"]

mixed.remove(True)
print(mixed) # [9, 2.71, False]

last_number = numbers.pop()
print(last_number) # 6
print(numbers) # [10, 20, 30, 4, 5]

first_name = names.pop(0)
print(first_name) # "Alice"
print(names) # ["Bob", "Eve", "David"]
```

```
print(mixed.index(2.71)) # 1
print(names.count("Bob")) # 1

numbers.extend([7, 8, 9])
print(numbers) # [10, 20, 30, 4, 5, 7, 8, 9]

names.clear()
print(names) # []
```

## List Comprehensions

A list comprehension is a concise and elegant way to create a new list from an existing iterable, such as another list, a range, a string, etc. A list comprehension consists of an expression that defines the elements of the new list, followed by a for clause that iterates over the iterable, and optionally one or more if clauses that filter the elements based on some condition. The general syntax of a list comprehension is:

```
[expression for element in iterable if condition]
```

For example, suppose we want to create a new list that contains the squares of the even numbers from 0 to 10. We can use a list comprehension as follows:

```
# Using a list comprehension to create a new list
squares = [n**2 for n in range(11) if n % 2 == 0]
print(squares) # [0, 4, 16, 36, 64, 100]
```

The expression `n**2` defines the elements of the new list, the for clause `for n in range(11)` iterates over the numbers from 0 to 10, and the if clause `if n % 2 == 0` filters only the even numbers.

List comprehensions can also use multiple for clauses to create nested loops, or multiple if clauses to create complex conditions. For example, suppose we want to create a new list that contains the products of the numbers from 1 to 3 and the numbers from 4 to 6. We can use a list comprehension with two for clauses as follows:

```
# Using a list comprehension with two for clauses
products = [x * y for x in range(1, 4) for y in range(4, 7)]
print(products) # [4, 5, 6, 8, 10, 12, 12, 15, 18]
```

The expression `x * y` defines the elements of the new list, the first for clause `for x in range(1, 4)` iterates over the numbers from 1 to 3, and the second for clause `for y in range(4, 7)` iterates over the numbers from 4 to 6 for each value of x.

Suppose we want to create a new list that contains the prime numbers from 2 to 20. We can use a list comprehension with two if clauses as follows:

```
# Using a list comprehension with two if clauses
primes = [n for n in range(2, 21) if all(n % d != 0 for d in range(2, n))]
print(primes) # [2, 3, 5, 7, 11, 13, 17, 19]
```

The expression `n` defines the elements of the new list, the first for clause `for n in range(2, 21)` iterates over the numbers from 2 to 20, and the first if clause `if all(n % d != 0 for d in range(2, n))` filters only the numbers that are not divisible by any number from 2 to n-1. The second for clause `for d in range(2, n)` and the second if clause `n % d != 0` are part of the expression `all()`, which returns True if all the elements of the iterable are True, and False otherwise.

List comprehensions are a powerful and concise way to create new lists from existing iterables, but they should be used with caution and readability in mind. Sometimes, a simple loop or a function may be more clear and appropriate than a complex list comprehension.

# Tuple

A tuple is an immutable, ordered, and heterogeneous sequence of values in Python. A tuple can contain any type of data, such as numbers, strings, booleans, or even other tuples. A tuple is created by enclosing the values in parentheses `( )`, separated by commas. For example:

```
# A tuple of numbers
numbers = (1, 2, 3, 4, 5)

# A tuple of strings
names = ("Alice", "Bob", "Charlie")

# A tuple of mixed types
mixed = (True, 3.14, "Hello", (6, 7, 8))
```

## Indexing and Slicing Tuples

To access a single element from a tuple, you can use the index operator `[ ]` with the index of the element inside. The index starts from 0 for the first element and goes up to the length of the tuple minus one for the last element. You can also use negative indices to access elements from the end of the tuple, starting from -1 for the last element and going down to -length for the first element.

For example:

```
# Accessing the first element
first = numbers[0] # 1

# Accessing the last element
last = names[-1] # "Charlie"

# Accessing the second element from the end
second_last = mixed[-2] # "Hello"
```

To access a range of elements from a tuple, you can use the slice operator `[ ]` with the start and end indices separated by a colon `:`. The slice will include the element at the start index and exclude the element at the end index. You can also omit the start or end index to indicate the beginning or the end of the tuple, respectively.

For example:

```
# Slicing the first three elements
first_three = numbers[0:3] # (1, 2, 3)

# Slicing the last two elements
last_two = names[-2:] # ("Bob", "Charlie")

# Slicing the middle two elements
middle_two = mixed[1:3] # (3.14, "Hello")
```

## Immutability and Hashing of Tuples

One of the key properties of tuples is that they are immutable, meaning that you cannot change their elements without creating a new tuple. You cannot use the assignment operator = to modify an element or a slice of a tuple.

For example:

```
# Trying to modify the first element
numbers[0] = 10
# TypeError: 'tuple' object does not support item assignment

# Trying to modify the last two elements
names[-2:] = ("David", "Eve")
# TypeError: 'tuple' object does not support item assignment

# Trying to modify the middle two elements
mixed[1:3] = (False, 2.71)
# TypeError: 'tuple' object does not support item assignment
```

However, this also means that tuples can be used as keys in dictionaries or elements in sets, as they are hashable, meaning that they have a unique value that can be used to identify them.

For example:

```
# Using tuples as keys in a dictionary
coordinates = {(0, 0): "Origin", (1, 1): "Point A", (2, 3):
"Point B"}
print(coordinates[(0, 0)]) # "Origin"
print(coordinates[(1, 1)]) # "Point A"
print(coordinates[(2, 3)]) # "Point B"

# Using tuples as elements in a set
colors = {("red", "green", "blue"), ("yellow", "magenta",
"cyan"), ("black", "white")}
print(("red", "green", "blue") in colors) # True
print(("orange", "purple", "pink") in colors) # False
```

However, note that a tuple can only be hashable if all its elements are hashable as well. For example, a tuple that contains a list cannot be used as a key in a dictionary or an element in a set, as lists are not hashable.

For example:

```
# Trying to use a tuple that contains a list as a key in a
dictionary
grades = {("Alice", [90, 80, 70]): "Pass", ("Bob", [60, 50,
40]): "Fail"}
# TypeError: unhashable type: 'list'

# Trying to use a tuple that contains a list as an element in
a set
numbers = {(1, 2, 3), (4, 5, [6, 7, 8])}
# TypeError: unhashable type: 'list'
```

## Built-in Functions and Methods for Tuples

Python provides some built-in functions and methods that can be used to perform various operations on tuples. Some of the most common ones are:

- `len(tuple)` returns the number of elements in a tuple
- `min(tuple)` returns the smallest element in a tuple
- `max(tuple)` returns the largest element in a tuple
- `sum(tuple)` returns the sum of all the elements in a tuple
- `sorted(tuple)` returns a new list with the elements sorted in ascending order
- `reversed(tuple)` returns a reversed iterator over the elements of a tuple
- `tuple.index(element)` returns the index of the first occurrence of an element in a tuple
- `tuple.count(element)` returns the number of times an element appears in a tuple

For example:

```
names = ("Alice", "Eve", "David")
mixed = (9, 2.71, False, True)
numbers = (10, 20, 30, 4, 5, 6)
# Using some built-in functions and methods on tuples
print(len(numbers)) # 6
print(min(names)) # "Alice"
print(max(mixed)) # 9
print(sum(numbers)) # 75
print(sorted(names)) # ["Alice", "David", "Eve"]
print(list(reversed(mixed))) # [True, False, 2.71, 9]
print(numbers.index(30)) # 2
print(names.count("Eve")) # 1
```

# Dictionaries

A dictionary is a mutable, unordered, and heterogeneous collection of key-value pairs in Python. A dictionary can store any type of data as values, such as numbers, strings, booleans, or even other dictionaries. However, the keys must be hashable, meaning that they have a unique value that can be used to identify them. A dictionary is created by enclosing the key-value pairs in curly braces `{ }`, separated by commas. Each key-value pair is written as `key: value`.

For example:

```
# A dictionary of numbers
numbers = {1: "One", 2: "Two", 3: "Three"}

# A dictionary of strings
names = {"Alice": "Smith", "Bob": "Jones", "Charlie":
"Brown"}

# A dictionary of mixed types
mixed = {True: 1, 3.14: "Pi", "Hello": [4, 5, 6], (7, 8, 9):
"Tuple"}
```

## Accessing and Modifying Dictionaries

To access a value from a dictionary, you can use the index operator `[ ]` with the key of the value inside. If the key is not present in the dictionary, a `KeyError` will be raised.

For example:

```
# Accessing a value by its key
print(numbers[1]) # "One"
print(names["Alice"]) # "Smith"
print(mixed[3.14]) # "Pi"

# Trying to access a value by a non-existent key
print(numbers[4])
# KeyError: 4
```

To modify a value in a dictionary, you can use the assignment operator = with the key of the value and the new value. If the key is already present in the dictionary, the old value will be replaced by the new value. If the key is not present in the dictionary, a new key-value pair will be added to the dictionary.

For example:

```
# Modifying a value by its key
numbers[1] = "One"
names["Alice"] = "Miller"
```

```
mixed[3.14] = "Pie"
print(numbers) # {1: "One", 2: "Two", 3: "Three"}
print(names) # {"Alice": "Miller", "Bob": "Jones", "Charlie":
"Brown"}
print(mixed) # {True: 1, 3.14: "Pie", "Hello": [4, 5, 6], (7,
8, 9): "Tuple"}

# Adding a new key-value pair
numbers[4] = "Four"
names["David"] = "Wilson"
mixed[False] = 0
print(numbers) # {1: "One", 2: "Two", 3: "Three", 4: "Four"}
print(names) # {"Alice": "Miller", "Bob": "Jones", "Charlie":
"Brown", "David": "Wilson"}
print(mixed) # {True: 1, 3.14: "Pie", "Hello": [4, 5, 6], (7,
8, 9): "Tuple", False: 0}
```

## Built-in Functions and Methods for Dictionaries

Python provides some built-in functions and methods that can be used to perform various operations on dictionaries. Some of the most common ones are:

- `len(dictionary)` returns the number of key-value pairs in a dictionary
- `keys(dictionary)` returns a view object that contains the keys of the dictionary
- `values(dictionary)` returns a view object that contains the values of the dictionary
- `items(dictionary)` returns a view object that contains the key-value pairs of the dictionary
- `dictionary.get(key, default)` returns the value of the key if it is present in the dictionary, otherwise returns the default value
- `dictionary.setdefault(key, default)` returns the value of the key if it is present in the dictionary, otherwise inserts the key with the default value and returns it
- `dictionary.update(other)` updates the dictionary with the key-value pairs from another dictionary or an iterable of key-value

pairs

- `dictionary.pop(key, default)` removes and returns the value of the key if it is present in the dictionary, otherwise returns the default value
- `dictionary.popitem()` removes and returns the last inserted key-value pair from the dictionary
- `dictionary.clear()` removes all the key-value pairs from the dictionary

For example:

```
s
# A dictionary of numbers
numbers = {1: "One", 2: "Two", 3: "Three"}

# A dictionary of strings
names = {"Alice": "Smith", "Bob": "Jones", "Charlie":
"Brown"}

# A dictionary of mixed types
mixed = {True: 1, 3.14: 5, 6: [4, 5, 6], (7, 8, 9): "Tuple"}

# Using some built-in functions and methods on dictionaries
print(len(numbers)) # 3
print(min(names)) # "Alice"
print(max(numbers)) # 3

print(list(numbers.keys())) # [1, 2, 3]
print(list(names.values())) # ['Smith', 'Jones', 'Brown']
print(list(mixed.items())) # [(True, 1), (3.14, 5), (6, [4,
5, 6]), ((7, 8, 9), 'Tuple')

print(numbers.get(5, "Five")) # "Five"
print(names.setdefault("Eve", "Green")) # "Green"
print(mixed.update({(10, 11, 12): "Tuple 2"}))
print(mixed) # {True: 1, 3.14: 5, 6: [4, 5, 6], (7, 8, 9):
'Tuple', (10, 11, 12): 'Tuple 2'}}

print(numbers.pop(4, "Four")) # "Four"
print(names.popitem()) # ("Eve", "Green")
print(mixed.clear())
print(mixed) # {}
```

# Set

A set is a mutable, unordered, and heterogeneous collection of unique and hashable values in Python. A set can store any type of data as long as it is hashable, meaning that it has a unique value that can be used to identify it. A set is created by enclosing the values in curly braces `{ }`, separated by commas, or by using the built-in function `set()`.

For example:

```
# A set of numbers
numbers = {1, 2, 3, 4, 5}

# A set of strings
names = {"Alice", "Bob", "Charlie"}

# A set of mixed types
mixed = {True, 3.14, "Hello", (6, 7, 8)}

# A set created by using the set function
colors = set(["red", "green", "blue"])
```

## Adding and Removing Elements from Sets

To add an element to a set, you can use the method `.add(element)`. If the element is already present in the set, it will have no effect.

For example:

```
# Adding an element to a set
numbers.add(6)
print(numbers) # {1, 2, 3, 4, 5, 6}

# Adding an element that is already present
names.add("Alice")
print(names) # {"Alice", "Bob", "Charlie"}
```

To remove an element from a set, you can use the method `.remove(element)`. If the element is not present in the set, a `KeyError` will be raised. Alternatively, you can use the method `.discard(element)`, which will silently ignore the element if it is not present in the set.

For example:

```
# Removing an element from a set
numbers.remove(6)
print(numbers) # {1, 2, 3, 4, 5}

# Removing an element that is not present
names.remove("David")
# KeyError: "David"

# Discarding an element that if it is present
mixed.discard(False)
print(mixed) # {True, 3.14, "Hello", (6, 7, 8)}
```

To remove and return an arbitrary element from a set, you can use the method `.pop()`. If the set is empty, a `KeyError` will be raised.

For example:

```
# Popping an element from a set
number = numbers.pop()
print(number) # 1
print(numbers) # {2, 3, 4, 5}

# Popping an element from an empty set
colors.clear()
color = colors.pop()
# KeyError: "pop from an empty set"
```

To remove all the elements from a set, you can use the method `.clear()`.

For example:

```
# Clearing a set
names.clear()
print(names) # set()
```

## Set Operations and Methods

Python provides some operators and methods that can be used to perform various operations on sets, such as union, intersection, difference, symmetric difference, subset, superset, and disjoint. Some of the most common ones are:

- `set1 | set2` or `set1.union(set2)` returns a new set that contains the elements that are in either set1 or set2, or both
- `set1 & set2` or `set1.intersection(set2)` returns a new set

that contains the elements that are in both set1 and set2

- `set1 - set2` or `set1.difference(set2)` returns a new set that contains the elements that are in set1 but not in set2
- `set1 ^ set2` or `set1.symmetric_difference(set2)` returns a new set that contains the elements that are in either set1 or set2, but not both
- `set1 <= set2` or `set1.issubset(set2)` returns True if set1 is a subset of set2, meaning that every element of set1 is also in set2
- `set1 >= set2` or `set1.issuperset(set2)` returns True if set1 is a superset of set2, meaning that every element of set2 is also in set1
- `set1.isdisjoint(set2)` returns True if set1 and set2 are disjoint, meaning that they have no elements in common
- For example:

```
# Using some set operations and methods on sets
print(numbers | names) # {1, 2, 3, 4, 5, "Alice", "Bob",
"Charlie"}
print(numbers.union(names)) # {1, 2, 3, 4, 5, "Alice", "Bob",
"Charlie"}

print(numbers & mixed) # {True}
print(numbers.intersection(mixed)) # {True}

print(numbers - mixed) # {2, 3, 4, 5}
print(numbers.difference(mixed)) # {2, 3, 4, 5}

print(numbers ^ mixed) # {2, 3, 4, 5, 3.14, "Hello", (6, 7,
8)}
print(numbers.symmetric_difference(mixed)) # {2, 3, 4, 5,
3.14, "Hello", (6, 7, 8)}

print(numbers <= mixed) # False
print(numbers.issubset(mixed)) # False

print(numbers >= mixed) # False
print(numbers.issuperset(mixed)) # False

print(numbers.isdisjoint(names)) # True
```

# Deque

A deque is a mutable, ordered, and heterogeneous sequence of values in Python that supports efficient insertion and deletion at both ends. A deque can contain any type of data, such as numbers, strings, booleans, or even other deques. A deque is created by using the `deque()` function from the collections module, which takes an optional iterable as an argument.

For example:

```
# Importing the collections module
import collections

# A deque of numbers
numbers = collections.deque([1, 2, 3, 4, 5])

# A deque of strings
names = collections.deque(["Alice", "Bob", "Charlie"])

# A deque of mixed types
mixed = collections.deque([True, 3.14, "Hello",
collections.deque([6, 7, 8])])
```

## Indexing and Slicing Deques

To access a single element from a deque, you can use the index operator `[ ]` with the index of the element inside. The index starts from 0 for the first element and goes up to the length of the deque minus one for the last element. You can also use negative indices to access elements from the end of the deque, starting from -1 for the last element and going down to -length for the first element.

For example:

```
# Accessing the first element
first = numbers[0] # 1

# Accessing the last element
last = names[-1] # "Charlie"

# Accessing the second element from the end
second_last = mixed[-2] # "Hello"
```

## Mutability and Aliasing of Deques

You have to be careful when assigning a deque to another variable, as this will create an alias, or a reference to the same deque, rather than a copy. This means that any changes made to one variable will affect the other variable as well.

For example:

```
# Assigning a deque to another variable
numbers_copy = numbers
print(numbers_copy) # deque([10, 2, 3, 4, 5])

# Modifying the original deque
numbers[1] = 20
print(numbers) # deque([10, 20, 3, 4, 5])

# The alias is also modified
print(numbers_copy) # deque([10, 20, 3, 4, 5])
```

To avoid this, you can use the copy method `.copy()` or the slice operator `[ ]` with no arguments to create a shallow copy of a deque, which will have the same elements but be a different object.

For example:

```
# Creating a shallow copy of a deque
numbers_copy = numbers.copy()
print(numbers_copy) # deque([10, 20, 3, 4, 5])

# Modifying the original deque
numbers[2] = 30
print(numbers) # deque([10, 20, 30, 4, 5])

# The copy is not modified
print(numbers_copy) # deque([10, 20, 3, 4, 5])
```

However, note that a shallow copy will only copy the first level of the deque, and any nested deques will still be references to the same objects. To create a deep copy of a deque, which will recursively copy all the elements and nested deques, you can use the copy module and its deepcopy function.

For example:

```
# Importing the copy module
import copy
```

```
# Creating a deep copy of a deque
mixed_copy = copy.deepcopy(mixed)
print(mixed_copy) # deque([True, False, 2.71, deque([6, 7,
8])])

# Modifying the original deque
mixed[3][0] = 9
print(mixed) # deque([True, False, 2.71, deque([9, 7, 8])])

# The copy is not modified
print(mixed_copy) # deque([True, False, 2.71, deque([6, 7,
8])])
```

## Built-in Functions and Methods for Deques

Python provides some built-in functions and methods that can be used to perform various operations on deques. Some of the most common ones are:

- `len(deque)` returns the number of elements in a deque
- `min(deque)` returns the smallest element in a deque
- `max(deque)` returns the largest element in a deque
- `sum(deque)` returns the sum of all the elements in a deque
- `sorted(deque)` returns a new list with the elements sorted in ascending order
- `reversed(deque)` returns a reversed iterator over the elements of a deque
- `deque.append(element)` adds an element to the right end of a deque
- `deque.appendleft(element)` adds an element to the left end of a deque
- `deque.insert(index, element)` inserts an element at a given index in a deque
- `deque.remove(element)` removes the first occurrence of an element from a deque
- `deque.pop()` removes and returns the element at the right end of a

deque

- `deque.popleft()` removes and returns the element at the left end of a deque
- `deque.index(element)` returns the index of the first occurrence of an element in a deque
- `deque.count(element)` returns the number of times an element appears in a deque
- `deque.extend(iterable)` adds all the elements of an iterable to the right end of a deque
- `deque.extendleft(iterable)` adds all the elements of an iterable to the left end of a deque
- `deque.rotate(n)` rotates the deque n steps to the right, or -n steps to the left
- `deque.clear()` removes all the elements from a deque

For example:

```
import collections

# A deque of numbers
numbers = collections.deque([1, 2, 3, 4, 5])

# A deque of strings
names = collections.deque(["Alice", "Bob", "Charlie"])

# A deque of mixed types
mixed = collections.deque([True, 3.14, "Hello",
collections.deque([6, 7, 8])])

# Using some built-in functions and methods on deques
print(len(numbers)) # 5
print(min(names)) # "Alice"
print(max(numbers)) # 5
print(sum(numbers)) # 15
print(sorted(names)) # ['Alice', 'Bob', 'Charlie']
print(list(reversed(mixed))) # [deque([6, 7, 8]), 'Hello',
3.14, True]

print(numbers.count(3)) # 1
print(names.count("Bob")) # 1
```

```
numbers.extend([6, 7, 8])
print(numbers) # deque([10, 20, 30, 4, 5, 6, 7, 8])

names.extendleft(["Eve", "David"])
print(names) # deque(['David', 'Eve', 'Alice', 'Bob',
'Charlie'])

numbers.rotate(2)
print(numbers) # deque([7, 8, 1, 2, 3, 4, 5, 6])

names.rotate(-1)
print(names) # deque(['Eve', 'Alice', 'Bob', 'Charlie',
'David'])

mixed.clear()
print(mixed) # deque([])
```

# Converting Data Structures

Sometimes, you may need to convert one type of data structure to another, depending on your needs and preferences. Python provides some built-in functions and methods that can help you with this task. Some of the most common ones are:

- `list(iterable)` returns a new list with the elements of the iterable
- `tuple(iterable)` returns a new tuple with the elements of the iterable
- `dict(iterable)` returns a new dictionary with the key-value pairs of the iterable
- `set(iterable)` returns a new set with the elements of the iterable
- `deque(iterable)` returns a new deque with the elements of the iterable

For example:

```
# Converting a list to a tuple
numbers = [1, 2, 3, 4, 5]
numbers_tuple = tuple(numbers)
print(numbers_tuple) # (1, 2, 3, 4, 5)

# Converting a tuple to a list
```

```
names = ("Alice", "Bob", "Charlie")
names_list = list(names)
print(names_list) # ["Alice", "Bob", "Charlie"]

# Converting a list of key-value pairs to a dictionary
colors = [("red", "#FF0000"), ("green", "#00FF00"), ("blue",
"#0000FF")]
colors_dict = dict(colors)
print(colors_dict) # {"red": "#FF0000", "green": "#00FF00",
"blue": "#0000FF"}

# Converting a dictionary to a list of key-value pairs
fruits = {"apple": 1, "banana": 2, "cherry": 3}
fruits_list = list(fruits.items())
print(fruits_list) # [("apple", 1), ("banana", 2), ("cherry",
3)]

# Converting a list to a set
numbers = [1, 2, 3, 3, 4, 2, 4]
numbers_set = set(numbers)
print(numbers_set) # {1, 2, 3, 4}

# Converting a set to a list
names = {"Alice", "Bob", "Charlie"}
names_list = list(names)
print(names_list) # ["Alice", "Bob", "Charlie"]

# Converting a list to a deque
numbers = [1, 2, 3, 4, 5]
numbers_deque = collections.deque(numbers)
print(numbers_deque) # deque([1, 2, 3, 4, 5])

# Converting a deque to a list
names = collections.deque(["Alice", "Bob", "Charlie"])
names_list = list(names)
print(names_list) # ["Alice", "Bob", "Charlie"]
```

Note that when you convert a data structure to another, you may lose some information or functionality. For example, when you convert a list to a set, you lose the order and the duplicates of the elements. When you convert a dictionary to a list, you lose the ability to access the values by their keys. When you convert a deque to a list, you lose the ability to append and pop items from both ends efficiently. Therefore, you should always consider the trade-offs and the benefits of each data structure before converting them.

# Iterating over Data Structures

One of the most common tasks when working with data structures is to iterate over their elements, meaning to access and process each element one by one. Python provides some built-in functions and methods that can help you with this task. Some of the most common ones are:

- `for element in iterable` is a loop that iterates over the elements of an iterable, such as a list, a tuple, a dictionary, a set, or a deque, and executes a block of code for each element
- `iter(iterable)` returns an iterator object that can be used to iterate over the elements of an iterable, using the `next()` function or a loop
- `enumerate(iterable)` returns an iterator object that yields pairs of index and element for each element of an iterable, starting from 0 by default
- `zip(iterable1, iterable2, ...)` returns an iterator object that yields tuples of elements from each iterable, stopping when the shortest iterable is exhausted
- `map(function, iterable)` returns an iterator object that applies a function to each element of an iterable and yields the results
- `filter(function, iterable)` returns an iterator object that yields the elements of an iterable that satisfy a function, which returns True or False
- `reversed(iterable)` returns an iterator object that yields the elements of an iterable in reverse order
- `sorted(iterable)` returns a new list with the elements of an iterable sorted in ascending order

For example:

```
# Using a for loop to iterate over a list
numbers = [1, 2, 3, 4, 5]
for number in numbers:
    print(number) # 1, 2, 3, 4, 5

# Using an iterator object to iterate over a tuple
names = ("Alice", "Bob", "Charlie")
names_iterator = iter(names)
```

```
print(next(names_iterator)) # "Alice"
print(next(names_iterator)) # "Bob"
print(next(names_iterator)) # "Charlie"
# print(next(names_iterator))
# StopIteration

# Using enumerate to iterate over a dictionary
fruits = {"apple": 1, "banana": 2, "cherry": 3}
for index, key in enumerate(fruits):
    print(index, key, fruits[key]) # 0 apple 1, 1 banana 2, 2
cherry 3

# Using zip to iterate over multiple iterables
colors = ["red", "green", "blue"]
codes = ["#FF0000", "#00FF00", "#0000FF"]
for color, code in zip(colors, codes):
    print(color, code) # red #FF0000, green #00FF00, blue
#0000FF

# Using map to apply a function to each element of an
iterable
numbers = [1, 2, 3, 4, 5]
squares = map(lambda x: x**2, numbers)
print(list(squares)) # [1, 4, 9, 16, 25]

# Using filter to select the elements of an iterable that
satisfy a condition
names = ["Alice", "Bob", "Charlie", "David", "Eve"]
long_names = filter(lambda x: len(x) > 4, names)
print(list(long_names)) # ["Alice", "Charlie", "David"]

# Using reversed to iterate over an iterable in reverse order
numbers = [1, 2, 3, 4, 5]
for number in reversed(numbers):
    print(number) # 5, 4, 3, 2, 1

# Using sorted to iterate over an iterable in sorted order
names = ["Alice", "Bob", "Charlie", "David", "Eve"]
for name in sorted(names):
    print(name) # Alice, Bob, Charlie, David, Eve
```

Note that when you iterate over a data structure, you should avoid modifying it, as this may lead to unexpected results or errors. For example, if you try to add or remove elements from a list while iterating over it, you may skip or repeat some elements, or raise an error. If you need to modify a data structure while iterating over it, you should make a copy of it first, or use a different data structure that supports concurrent modification, such as a deque.

# Transformations

Sometimes, you may need to apply some transformations on data structures, such as reversing, sorting, or shuffling their elements. Python provides some built-in functions and methods that can help you with this task. Some of the most common ones are:

- `reversed(iterable)` returns a reversed iterator over the elements of an iterable, such as a list, a tuple, a dictionary, a set, or a deque
- `iterable.reverse()` reverses the elements of the iterable in place, if the iterable has this method
- `sorted(iterable)` returns a new list with the elements of the iterable sorted in ascending order
- `iterable.sort()` sorts the elements of the iterable in place, if the iterable has this method
- `random.shuffle(iterable)` shuffles the elements of the iterable randomly, if the iterable is mutable and supports indexing
- `random.sample(iterable, k)` returns a new list with k elements randomly chosen from the iterable, without replacement

For example:

```
# Importing the random module
import random

# Using reversed to reverse the order of a list
numbers = [1, 2, 3, 4, 5]
numbers_reversed = reversed(numbers)
print(list(numbers_reversed)) # [5, 4, 3, 2, 1]

# Using reverse to reverse the order of a deque
names = collections.deque(["Alice", "Bob", "Charlie"])
names.reverse()
print(names) # deque(["Charlie", "Bob", "Alice"])

# Using sorted to sort the elements of a tuple
fruits = ("apple", "banana", "cherry")
```

```
fruits_sorted = sorted(fruits)
print(fruits_sorted) # ["apple", "banana", "cherry"]

# Using sort to sort the elements of a list
colors = ["red", "green", "blue"]
colors.sort()
print(colors) # ["blue", "green", "red"]

# Using shuffle to shuffle the elements of a list
numbers = [1, 2, 3, 4, 5]
random.shuffle(numbers)
print(numbers) # [3, 5, 4, 1, 2]

# Using sample to select a random subset of a set
names = {"Alice", "Bob", "Charlie", "David", "Eve"}
names_sample = random.sample(sorted(names), 3)
print(names_sample) # ["Charlie", "Alice", "Eve"]
```

Note that when you apply transformations on data structures, you may change their properties or functionality. For example, when you reverse a list, you change its order and indexing. When you sort a set, you lose its uniqueness and hashing. When you shuffle a dictionary, you lose its key-value association. Therefore, you should always consider the trade-offs and the benefits of each transformation before applying them.

# Nested Data Structures

A nested data structure is a data structure that contains another data structure as its element, such as a list of lists, a tuple of tuples, a dictionary of dictionaries, etc. A nested data structure can be useful for storing and organizing complex or hierarchical data, such as matrices, graphs, trees, etc.

For example:

```
# A list of lists that represents a matrix
matrix = [[1, 2, 3], [4, 5, 6], [7, 8, 9]]

# A tuple of tuples that represents a pair of coordinates
coordinates = ((0, 0), (1, 1), (2, 3))

# A dictionary of dictionaries that represents a graph
graph = {"A": {"B": 1, "C": 2}, "B": {"A": 1, "D": 3}, "C":
{"A": 2, "D": 4}, "D": {"B": 3, "C": 4}}
```

## Accessing and Modifying Nested Data Structures

To access an element from a nested data structure, you can use the index operator [ ] with the indices of the element inside, separated by commas. The indices start from 0 for the first element and go up to the length of the data structure minus one for the last element. You can also use negative indices to access elements from the end of the data structure, starting from -1 for the last element and going down to -length for the first element.

For example:

```
# Accessing an element from a list of lists
print(matrix[0][0]) # 1
print(matrix[1][2]) # 6
print(matrix[-1][-1]) # 9

# Accessing an element from a tuple of tuples
print(coordinates[0][0]) # 0
print(coordinates[1][1]) # 1
print(coordinates[-1][-1]) # 3

# Accessing an element from a dictionary of dictionaries
print(graph["A"]["B"]) # 1
print(graph["B"]["D"]) # 3
print(graph["D"]["C"]) # 4
```

To modify an element in a nested data structure, you can use the assignment operator = with the indices of the element and the new value. However, this only works if the data structure is mutable, such as a list or a dictionary. If the data structure is immutable, such as a tuple, you cannot modify its elements without creating a new data structure.

For example:

```
# Modifying an element in a list of lists
matrix[0][0] = 10
print(matrix) # [[10, 2, 3], [4, 5, 6], [7, 8, 9]]

# Modifying an element in a dictionary of dictionaries
graph["A"]["B"] = 5
print(graph) # {"A": {"B": 5, "C": 2}, "B": {"A": 1, "D": 3},
"C": {"A": 2, "D": 4}, "D": {"B": 3, "C": 4}}

# Trying to modify an element in a tuple of tuples
coordinates[0][0] = 10
# TypeError: 'tuple' object does not support item assignment
```

## Built-in Functions and Methods for Nested Data Structures

Python provides some built-in functions and methods that can be used to perform various operations on nested data structures, such as creating, copying, flattening, or traversing them. Some of the most common ones are:

- `list(iterable)` returns a new list with the elements of the iterable, which can be another list or a nested data structure
- `tuple(iterable)` returns a new tuple with the elements of the iterable, which can be another tuple or a nested data structure
- `dict(iterable)` returns a new dictionary with the key-value pairs of the iterable, which can be another dictionary or a nested data structure
- `copy.copy(object)` returns a shallow copy of the object, which can be a data structure or a nested data structure
- `copy.deepcopy(object)` returns a deep copy of the object, which can be a data structure or a nested data structure
- `itertools.chain(*iterables)` returns an iterator that chains the elements of the iterables, which can be data structures or nested data structures
- `itertools.chain.from_iterable(iterable)` returns an iterator that chains the elements of the iterable, which can be a nested data structure
- `itertools.product(*iterables)` returns an iterator that yields the Cartesian product of the iterables, which can be data structures or nested data structures
- `itertools.combinations(iterable, r)` returns an iterator that yields the r-length combinations of the elements of the iterable, which can be a data structure or a nested data structure
- `itertools.permutations(iterable, r)` returns an iterator that yields the r-length permutations of the elements of the iterable, which can be a data structure or a nested data structure
- `itertools.accumulate(iterable, func)` returns an iterator that yields the accumulated results of applying the function to the elements of the iterable, which can be a data structure or a nested data

structure

- `itertools.groupby(iterable, key)` returns an iterator that yields the key and a group iterator for each group of consecutive elements that have the same key, which can be a data structure or a nested data structure
- `itertools.islice(iterable, start, stop, step)` returns an iterator that yields the selected elements of the iterable, which can be a data structure or a nested data structure
- `itertools.starmap(function, iterable)` returns an iterator that applies the function to each element of the iterable, which can be a nested data structure
- `itertools.zip_longest(*iterables, fillvalue)` returns an iterator that yields tuples of elements from the iterables, which can be data structures or nested data structures, filling the missing values with the fillvalue
- `itertools.tee(iterable, n)` returns n independent iterators that yield the elements of the iterable, which can be a data structure or a nested data structure

For example:

```
# Importing the copy and itertools modules
import copy
import itertools

# Creating a list of lists from a tuple of tuples
coordinates = ((0, 0), (1, 1), (2, 3))
matrix = list(coordinates)
print(matrix) # [(0, 0), (1, 1), (2, 3)]

# Creating a tuple of tuples from a list of lists
matrix = [[1, 2, 3], [4, 5, 6], [7, 8, 9]]
coordinates = tuple(matrix)
print(coordinates) # ([1, 2, 3], [4, 5, 6], [7, 8, 9])

# Creating a dictionary of dictionaries from a list of key-
value pairs
colors = [("red", "#FF0000"), ("green", "#00FF00"), ("blue",
"#0000FF")]
codes = dict(colors)
```

```
print(codes) # {"red": "#FF0000", "green": "#00FF00", "blue":
"#0000FF"}

# Creating a list of key-value pairs from a dictionary of
dictionaries
fruits = {"apple": 1, "banana": 2, "cherry": 3}
prices = list(fruits.items())
print(prices) # [("apple", 1), ("banana", 2), ("cherry", 3)]

# Creating a shallow copy of a list of lists
matrix = [[1, 2, 3], [4, 5, 6], [7, 8, 9]]
matrix_copy = copy.copy(matrix)
print(matrix_copy) # [[1, 2, 3], [4, 5, 6], [7, 8, 9]]

# Creating a deep copy of a list of lists
matrix = [[1, 2, 3], [4, 5, 6], [7, 8, 9]]
matrix_copy = copy.deepcopy(matrix)
print(matrix_copy) # [[1, 2, 3], [4, 5, 6], [7, 8, 9]]

# Flattening a list of lists using chain
matrix = [[1, 2, 3], [4, 5, 6], [7, 8, 9]]
flat_matrix = itertools.chain(*matrix)
print(list(flat_matrix)) # [1, 2, 3, 4, 5, 6, 7, 8, 9]

# Flattening a list of lists using chain.from_iterable
matrix = [[1, 2, 3], [4, 5, 6], [7, 8, 9]]
flat_matrix = itertools.chain.from_iterable(matrix)
print(list(flat_matrix)) # [1, 2, 3, 4, 5, 6, 7, 8, 9]

# Creating the Cartesian product of two lists of lists using
product
matrix1 = [[1, 2, 3], [4, 5, 6]]
matrix2 = [[7, 8, 9], [10, 11, 12]]
product_matrix = itertools.product(matrix1, matrix2)
print(list(product_matrix))

# Creating the permutations of a list using permutations
numbers = [1, 2, 3, 4, 5]
permutations_numbers = itertools.permutations(numbers, 3)
print(list(permutations_numbers))
# [(1, 2, 3), (1, 2, 4), (1, 2, 5), (1, 3, 2), (1, 3, 4), (1,
3, 5), (1, 4, 2), (1, 4, 3), (1, 4, 5), (1, 5, 2), (1, 5, 3),
(1, 5, 4), (2, 1, 3), (2, 1, 4), (2, 1, 5), (2, 3, 1), (2, 3,
4), (2, 3, 5), (2, 4, 1), (2, 4, 3), (2, 4, 5), (2, 5, 1),
(2, 5, 3), (2, 5, 4), (3, 1, 2), (3, 1, 4), (3, 1, 5), (3, 2,
1), (3, 2, 4), (3, 2, 5), (3, 4, 1), (3, 4, 2), (3, 4, 5),
(3, 5, 1), (3, 5, 2), (3, 5, 4), (4, 1, 2), (4, 1, 3), (4, 1,
```

```
5), (4, 2, 1), (4, 2, 3), (4, 2, 5), (4, 3, 1), (4, 3, 2),
(4, 3, 5), (4, 5, 1), (4, 5, 2), (4, 5, 3), (5, 1, 2), (5, 1,
3), (5, 1, 4), (5, 2, 1), (5, 2, 3), (5, 2, 4), (5, 3, 1),
(5, 3, 2), (5, 3, 4), (5, 4, 1), (5, 4, 2), (5, 4, 3)]

# Creating the accumulated results of applying a function to
a list using accumulate
numbers = [1, 2, 3, 4, 5]
factorials = itertools.accumulate(numbers, lambda x, y: x *
y)
print(list(factorials)) # [1, 2, 6, 24, 120]

# Creating the groups of consecutive elements that have the
same # length using groupby
names = ["Alice", "Bob", "Charlie", "David", "Eve"]
names_by_length = itertools.groupby(names, len)
for length, group in names_by_length:
    print(length, list(group)) # 5 ["Alice"], 3 ["Bob"], 7
["Charlie"], 5 ["David"], 3 ["Eve"]

# Creating the selected elements of a list using islice
numbers = [1, 2, 3, 4, 5, 6, 7, 8, 9]
odd_numbers = itertools.islice(numbers, 0, None, 2)
print(list(odd_numbers)) # [1, 3, 5, 7, 9]

# Applying a function to each element of a list of lists
using starmap
def summa(*numbers):
    result = 0
    for i in numbers:
        result += i
    return result
matrix = [[1, 2, 3], [4, 5, 6], [7, 8, 9]]
sums = itertools.starmap(summa, matrix)
print(list(sums)) # [6, 15, 24]

# Creating tuples of elements from two lists using
zip_longest
colors = ["red", "green", "blue"]
codes = ["#FF0000", "#00FF00"]
colors_codes = itertools.zip_longest(colors, codes,
fillvalue="N/A")
print(list(colors_codes)) # [("red", "#FF0000"), ("green",
"#00FF00"), ("blue", "N/A")]

# Creating independent iterators from a list using tee
numbers = [1, 2, 3, 4, 5]
```

```
numbers_iter1, numbers_iter2 = itertools.tee(numbers, 2)
print(list(numbers_iter1)) # [1, 2, 3, 4, 5]
print(list(numbers_iter2)) # [1, 2, 3, 4, 5]
```

# Comprehensions

A comprehension is a concise way to create a new data structure from an existing iterable, such as a list, a tuple, a dictionary, a set, or a deque, by applying some transformation or filtering on its elements. Python supports four types of comprehensions: list comprehensions, tuple comprehensions, dictionary comprehensions, and set comprehensions. A comprehension consists of an expression that defines the elements of the new data structure, followed by a for clause that iterates over the elements of the iterable, and optionally one or more if clauses that filter the elements based on some condition. The general syntax of a comprehension is:

```
[data_structure(expression) for element in iterable if
condition]
```

For example:

- A list comprehension creates a new list from an iterable. For example, suppose we want to create a new list that contains the squares of the numbers from 0 to 10. We can use a list comprehension as follows:

```
# Using a list comprehension to create a new list
squares = [n**2 for n in range(11)]
print(squares) # [0, 1, 4, 9, 16, 25, 36, 49, 64, 81, 100]
```

- A tuple comprehension creates a new tuple from an iterable. However, unlike a list comprehension, a tuple comprehension requires parentheses around the expression and the for clause. For example, suppose we want to create a new tuple that contains the cubes of the numbers from 0 to 10. We can use a tuple comprehension as follows:

```
# Using a tuple comprehension to create a new tuple
cubes = tuple((n**3 for n in range(11)))
print(cubes) # (0, 1, 8, 27, 64, 125, 216, 343, 512, 729,
1000)
```

- A dictionary comprehension creates a new dictionary from an iterable. The expression must consist of a key-value pair, separated by a colon. For example, suppose we want to create a new dictionary that maps the numbers from 0 to 10 to their squares. We can use a dictionary comprehension as follows:

```
# Using a dictionary comprehension to create a new dictionary
squares = {n: n**2 for n in range(11)}
print(squares) # {0: 0, 1: 1, 2: 4, 3: 9, 4: 16, 5: 25, 6:
36, 7: 49, 8: 64, 9: 81, 10: 100}
```

- A set comprehension creates a new set from an iterable. The expression must be hashable, meaning that it has a unique value that can be used to identify it. For example, suppose we want to create a new set that contains the unique words from a sentence. We can use a set comprehension as follows:

```
# Using a set comprehension to create a new set
sentence = "This is a sentence with some repeated words"
words = {word for word in sentence.split()}
print(words) # {"This", "is", "a", "sentence", "with",
"some", "repeated", "words"}
```

Comprehensions can also use multiple for clauses to create nested loops, or multiple if clauses to create complex conditions. For example, suppose we want to create a new list that contains the products of the numbers from 1 to 3 and the numbers from 4 to 6. We can use a list comprehension with two for clauses as follows:

```
# Using a list comprehension with two for clauses
products = [x * y for x in range(1, 4) for y in range(4, 7)]
print(products) # [4, 5, 6, 8, 10, 12, 12, 15, 18]
```

Suppose we want to create a new set that contains the prime numbers from 2 to 20. We can use a set comprehension with two if clauses as follows:

```
# Using a set comprehension with two if clauses
primes = {n for n in range(2, 21) if all(n % d != 0 for d in
range(2, n))}
print(primes) # {2, 3, 5, 7, 11, 13, 17, 19}
```

Comprehensions are a powerful and concise way to create new data structures from existing iterables, but they should be used with caution and readability in mind. Sometimes, a simple loop or a function may be more clear and appropriate than a complex comprehension.

# collections Data Types

## defaultdict

A `collections.defaultdict` is a subclass of `dict` that returns a default value for a missing key. It takes a function as an argument that provides the default value. For example, a `collections.defaultdict(int)` will return 0 for any missing key, and a `collections.defaultdict(list)` will return an empty list for any missing key. This is useful for creating dictionaries that store multiple values for each key, such as a list of words with their frequencies or a list of students with their grades.

For example:

```
# Import the collections module
import collections

# Create a defaultdict that returns an empty list for a
missing key
words = collections.defaultdict(list)

# Add some words and their frequencies to the defaultdict
words["apple"].append(3)
words["banana"].append(5)
words["cherry"].append(2)

# Print the defaultdict
print(words) #defaultdict(<class 'list'>, {'apple': [3],
'banana': [5], 'cherry': [2]})

# Print the frequency of a word that is in the defaultdict
print(words["apple"]) #[3]

# Print the frequency of a word that is not in the
defaultdict
print(words["dragon"]) []
```

## OrderedDict

An `OrderedDict` is a dictionary subclass that remembers the order in which its contents are added. This can be particularly useful when the order of elements needs to be preserved during iterations or serializations.

```
from collections import OrderedDict
```

```
# Create an OrderedDict and add items
ordered_dict = OrderedDict()
ordered_dict['one'] = 1
ordered_dict['two'] = 2
ordered_dict['three'] = 3

# The items will be printed in the order they were added
for key, value in ordered_dict.items():
    print(key, value) #one 1 two 2 three 3
```

## namedtuple

A `namedtuple` is a factory function for creating tuple subclasses with named fields. It provides a way to create tuple-like objects that have fields accessible by attribute lookup as well as being indexable and iterable.

```
from collections import namedtuple

# Create a namedtuple to represent a point in 2D space
Point = namedtuple('Point', ['x', 'y'])
p = Point(11, y=22)

# Accessing the fields
print(p[0] + p[1])  # Output: 33
print(p.x + p.y)    # Output: 33
```

## ChainMap

A `ChainMap` groups multiple dictionaries into a single, updateable view. If no dictionaries are specified, a single empty dictionary is provided.

```
from collections import ChainMap

dict1 = {'one': 1, 'two': 2}
dict2 = {'three': 3, 'four': 4}
chain_map = ChainMap(dict1, dict2)

print(chain_map['three'])  # Output: 3
```

### Counter

A `Counter` is a `dict` subclass for counting hashable objects. It is a collection where elements are stored as dictionary keys and their counts are stored as dictionary values.

```
from collections import Counter

# Create a Counter object
counter = Counter(['red', 'blue', 'red', 'green', 'blue',
'blue'])

print(counter)  # Output: Counter({'blue': 3, 'red': 2,
'green': 1})
```

In the context of data analysis and data science, stacks and queues can be particularly useful for managing data in a structured way.

## Stack

A stack is a data structure that follows the Last In, First Out (LIFO) principle. It's useful for tasks that require backtracking, such as parsing expressions or navigating through browser history.

You can implement a stack using a list or `collections.deque`. The list implementation is straightforward, with the `append()` method to push an item and the `pop()` method to pop an item.

```
# Stack implementation using a list
stack = []
stack.append('data1')
stack.append('data2')
print(stack.pop())  # Output: 'data2'
```

For larger datasets or performance-critical applications, `collections.deque` is more efficient.

```
from collections import deque

# Stack implementation using deque
stack = deque()
stack.append('data1')
stack.append('data2')
print(stack.pop())  # Output: 'data2'
```

# Queue

A queue operates on the First In, First Out (FIFO) principle. It's ideal for tasks that need to be processed in the order they were received, like task scheduling.

The `queue.Queue` class is a thread-safe FIFO implementation suitable for concurrent data processing.

```
from queue import Queue

# Queue implementation using queue.Queue
q = Queue()
q.put('data1')
q.put('data2')
print(q.get())  # Output: 'data1'
```

Alternatively, `collections.deque` can be used for a non-thread-safe implementation that's still very efficient.

```
from collections import deque

# Queue implementation using deque
queue = deque()
queue.append('data1')
queue.append('data2')
print(queue.popleft())  # Output: 'data1'
```

# Function

In Python, a function is a block of organized, reusable code that is used to perform a single, related action. Functions provide better modularity for your application.

Defining a function in Python involves using the `def` keyword, followed by a function name with parentheses and a colon. Inside the function, you can write the code that defines what the function does.

Here's an example of defining and calling a function that calculates the square of a number:

```
def square(number):
    """This function returns the square of the number passed
in as a parameter."""
    return number ** 2

# Calling the function
result = square(4)
print(result)  # Output: 16
```

In this example, `square` is the function that takes `number` as an argument and returns its square. We then call the function with `4` as the input, and it returns `16`.

Here's an example of defining and calling a function that print name:

```
def greet(name):
    """This function greets to the person passed in as a
parameter"""
    return f"Hello, {name}!"
```

You can then **call** the function with the appropriate parameter:

```
print(greet("Alice"))
```

This will output: `Hello, Alice!`

## Understand Scope

In Python, the scope of a variable determines the part of the program where you can access a particular identifier. There are two basic scopes of variables in Python - **global** and **local**.

- **Global variables** are defined outside of a function and can be accessed anywhere after they are declared.
- **Local variables** are defined inside a function and can only be used within that function.

Here's an example to illustrate scope:

```
x = "global"

def foo():
    y = "local"
    print("Inside function:", y)

foo()
print("Outside function:", x)
```

In this example, `y` is a local variable, and its scope is limited to the `foo()` function. `x` is a global variable, and it can be accessed both inside and outside of the `foo()` function.

## Global Scope

A variable that's defined in the main body of a Python script is a global variable and belongs to the global scope. Global variables are accessible from any point in the Python script, not just the block in which they are defined.

Here's an example:

```
# Global variable
global_var = "I am global"

def access_global():
    # Accessing the global variable
    print(global_var)

access_global()  # Output: I am global
print(global_var)  # Output: I am global
```

## Local Scope

A variable that's defined within a function belongs to the local scope of that function, and can only be used inside that function.

```
def define_local():
    # Local variable
    local_var = "I am local"
    print(local_var)

define_local()  # Output: I am local
print(local_var)  # This would raise an error because
local_var is not accessible here.
```

## Interaction Between Local and Global Scope

When you define a variable inside a function, it's local by default. When you define a variable outside all functions, it's global by default. If you need to use a global variable inside a function, you can do so using the `global` keyword.

```
# Global variable
global_var = "I am global"

def modify_global():
    global global_var
    global_var = "Modified global"

modify_global()
print(global_var)  # Output: Modified global
```

In this example, we modified the global variable `global_var` inside the `modify_global` function by first declaring it as global within the function.

## Shadowing Global Variables

If you define a local variable with the same name as a global variable, the local variable will "shadow" the global variable within the function's scope.

```
# Global variable
shadow_var = "Global shadow"

def shadowing_example():
    # Local variable with the same name as the global
variable
    shadow_var = "Local shadow"
    print(shadow_var)

shadowing_example()  # Output: Local shadow
print(shadow_var)  # Output: Global shadow
```

In this case, shadow_var inside the shadowing_example function is a separate entity from the shadow_var outside the function.

Understanding these concepts is crucial for managing and debugging variable values and their changes across different parts of your Python program.

# Nested Functions

A nested function, or inner function, is a function defined inside another function. The inner function is only in scope within the outer function, meaning it can be called only inside the outer function.

Here's an example:

```
def outer_function(x):
    def inner_function(y):
        return y * x
    return inner_function

# The inner_function can be accessed and called only inside
outer_function
double = outer_function(2)
print(double(5))  # Output: 10
```

In this example, inner_function is nested within outer_function. It multiplies its argument y by the parameter x of the outer function. The outer_function returns the inner_function, which we then call with 5.

## Scope in Nested Functions

The inner function has access to the variables defined in the enclosing scope of the outer function. This is known as a closure. However, it does not have access to the outer function's arguments and local variables unless they are passed to it or defined as nonlocal.

```
def outer_function(x):
    z = 3
    def inner_function(y):
        return y * x * z
    return inner_function

triple = outer_function(3)
print(triple(5))  # Output: 45
```

Here, `inner_function` uses both `x` and `z` from the outer function's scope.

### The `nonlocal` Keyword

If you want to modify a variable from the outer function within the inner function, you need to use the `nonlocal` keyword. This tells Python that the variable should not be treated as local to the inner function, allowing you to modify it.

```
def outer_function():
    x = "Hello"
    def inner_function():
        nonlocal x
        x = "Hi"
    inner_function()
    return x

print(outer_function())  # Output: Hi
```

In this example, inner_function modifies the x variable from the outer_function scope, changing its value from "Hello" to "Hi".

Nested functions can be useful for creating closures, which are functions that remember the values from their enclosing scopes, and for organizing code into more manageable, hierarchical structures.

## Arguments and Shared References

When you pass arguments to a function in Python, you are essentially passing references to the objects, not copies of the objects. This means that if you pass a mutable object (like a list or a dictionary) to a function, the function can modify that object in-place, and these changes will be reflected outside the function as well.

Here's an example to illustrate this:

```
def modify_list(lst):
    lst.append(100)

my_list = [1, 2, 3]
modify_list(my_list)
print(my_list)  # Output: [1, 2, 3, 100]
```

In this example, `modify_list` takes a list as an argument and appends the value `100` to it. Because lists are mutable, the change is reflected in the `my_list` variable outside the function.

## Immutable Objects

However, if you pass an immutable object (like an integer, float, string, or tuple) to a function, the function cannot change the original object. Instead, any changes will create a new object.

```
def modify_number(x):
    x += 10
    return x

num = 5
new_num = modify_number(num)
print(num)      # Output: 5
print(new_num)  # Output: 15
```

Here, `modify_number` attempts to modify the immutable integer `x`. The original `num` remains unchanged, while `new_num` holds the result of the operation.

## The `id` Function and Shared References

The `id` function in Python returns a unique identifier for an object, which can be used to determine if two variables point to the same object (shared reference).

```
a = [1, 2, 3]
b = a
print(id(a) == id(b))  # Output: True
```

In this case, `a` and `b` share a reference to the same list object, so their `id`s are equal.

## Copying Objects

To avoid unintended side effects of shared references, you can create copies of objects:

- Shallow copy: creates a new object, but fills it with references to the items found in the original.
- Deep copy: creates a new object and recursively adds copies of the objects

found in the original.

```
import copy

# Shallow copy
original_list = [[1, 2, 3], [4, 5, 6]]
shallow_copied_list = copy.copy(original_list)

# Deep copy
deep_copied_list = copy.deepcopy(original_list)
```

With a shallow copy, changes to mutable elements of the original list will affect the copy. With a deep copy, the two lists are completely independent.

# Argument Matching

Argument matching in Python refers to the way that arguments are assigned to parameters when a function is called. Understanding argument matching is crucial for writing functions that are both flexible and easy to use. Here are the key concepts:

## Positional Arguments

These are the most common and straightforward. When you call a function, Python matches each argument in the call to the corresponding parameter in the function definition based on their order.

```
def describe_pet(animal, name):
    print(f"I have a {animal} named {name}.")

describe_pet('hamster', 'Harry')
# Output: I have a hamster named Harry.
```

## Keyword Arguments

You can also call a function by explicitly specifying which argument goes with which parameter, regardless of their order, using the names of the parameters.

```
describe_pet(name='Harry', animal='hamster')
# Output: I have a hamster named Harry.
```

## Default Parameters

You can assign default values to parameters. If the argument is not provided in the call, the parameter uses the default value.

```
def describe_pet(name, animal='dog'):
    print(f"I have a {animal} named {name}.")

describe_pet(name='Bruno')
# Output: I have a dog named Bruno.
```

## Variable-length Arguments

Sometimes you might want to define a function that can accept any number of arguments. This is done using `*args` for non-keyword variable-length arguments and `**kwargs` for keyword variable-length arguments.

- `*args` is used to pass a variable number of non-keyword arguments to a function. It is like a tuple.
- `**kwargs` allows you to pass a variable number of keyword arguments to a function. It is like a dictionary.

```
def make_pizza(*toppings):
    print("Making a pizza with the following toppings:")
    for topping in toppings:
        print(f"- {topping}")

make_pizza('pepperoni')
make_pizza('mushrooms', 'green peppers', 'extra cheese')
```

## Combined Argument Types

You can combine positional, keyword, default, and variable-length arguments in a single function to provide more flexibility.

```
def make_smoothie(*fruits, **options):
    print("Making a smoothie with:")
    for fruit in fruits:
        print(f"- {fruit}")
    if options.get("sweetener"):
        print(f"Adding sweetener: {options['sweetener']}")

make_smoothie('banana', 'strawberries', sweetener='honey')
```

In this example, `*fruits` takes any number of fruit names, and `**options` takes any number of keyword arguments, which we used to specify a sweetener.

Understanding these different types of argument matching allows you to create functions that are both powerful and intuitive for users to call in various ways, depending on their needs.

# Decorators

Decorators are a very powerful and useful tool in Python since they allow you to modify the behavior of a function or class. Decorators are used to extend or alter the functionality of functions and methods without permanently modifying them.

## What is a Decorator?

A decorator is a function that takes another function and extends the behavior of the latter function without explicitly modifying it. It's a very powerful tool in Python because it allows for the addition of new functionality to an existing object without modifying its structure.

## How Do Decorators Work?

Decorators work by taking a function, adding some functionality to it, and returning it. In Python, functions are first-class objects, which means that they can be passed around and used as arguments, just like any other object (string, int, float, list, and so on).

Here's a simple example of a decorator that prints "Hello" before the execution of a function:

```
def my_decorator(func):
    def wrapper():
        print("Hello")
        func()
    return wrapper

@my_decorator
def say_welcome():
    print("Welcome to the world of decorators!")

say_welcome() # Output: Hello

# Welcome to the world of decorators!
```

## Common Uses of Decorators

- **Logging**: Decorators can be used to log information about function usage (like parameters and return values).
- **Timing**: They can measure the time a function takes to execute, which is useful for performance testing.
- **Authentication**: Decorators can enforce access control to certain parts of code.
- **Caching**: They can cache the results of function calls, so the same calculations don't have to be performed multiple times.

## Chaining Decorators

You can apply multiple decorators to a single function by stacking them on top of each other.

```
@decorator_one
@decorator_two
def my_function():
    pass
```

In this case, `decorator_two` will be applied to `my_function` first, and then `decorator_one` will be applied to the result.

Decorators are a key part of Python and are widely used in web frameworks like Flask and Django, as well as in many other contexts.

Decorators in Python are a very powerful feature that allow you to modify the behavior of functions or methods. Let's delve into some detailed examples to understand how decorators work and how they can be used.

## Simple Decorator Example

Here's a simple decorator that logs the execution of any function it decorates:

```
def log_decorator(func):
    def wrapper(*args, **kwargs):
        print(f"Executing {func.__name__}")
        result = func(*args, **kwargs)
        print(f"{func.__name__} finished execution")
        return result
    return wrapper
```

```
@log_decorator
def add(a, b):
    return a + b

print(add(3, 4)) # Output: Executing add

# add finished execution

#7
```

In this example, `log_decorator` is a decorator that prints a message before and after the execution of the function it decorates. The `add` function is decorated with `@log_decorator`, which means that when `add` is called, it's wrapped by the `wrapper` function inside `log_decorator`.

## Decorator with Arguments

Sometimes you might want to pass arguments to your decorator. Here's how you can create a decorator that accepts arguments:

```
def repeat(times):
    def decorator_repeat(func):
        def wrapper(*args, **kwargs):
            for _ in range(times):
                value = func(*args, **kwargs)
            return value
        return wrapper
    return decorator_repeat

@repeat(times=3)
def say_hello(name):
    print(f"Hello {name}")

say_hello("Alice") # Output:

# Hello Alice

# Hello Alice
# Hello Alice
```

In this example, `repeat` is a decorator factory that takes an argument `times`. It returns the actual decorator `decorator_repeat` which then takes the function to be decorated. The `wrapper` function inside `decorator_repeat` will execute the decorated function the number of times specified by `times`.

## Class Decorators

Decorators can also be applied to classes. Here's an example of a class decorator that adds a new method to the class:

```
def add_method(cls):
    cls.greet = lambda self: f"Hello, my name is {self.name}"
    return cls

@add_method
class Person:
    def __init__(self, name):
        self.name = name

p = Person("John")
print(p.greet()) # Output: Hello, my name is John
```

In this example, `add_method` is a class decorator that adds a `greet` method to any class it decorates. When we decorate the `Person` class with `@add_method`, we dynamically add the `greet` method to it.

These examples illustrate the flexibility and power of decorators in Python. They can be used to modify the behavior of functions and classes in a clean and readable way.

## Using decorators effectively

Let's go through the best practices for using decorators in Python with examples for each:

**1. Use `functools.wraps`:** This preserves the metadata of the original function when it is decorated.

```
from functools import wraps

def my_decorator(func):
    @wraps(func)
    def wrapper(*args, **kwargs):
        # Decorator logic
        return func(*args, **kwargs)
```

```
    return wrapper

@my_decorator
def my_function():
    """My function's docstring"""
    pass

print(my_function.__name__)  # Output: my_function
print(my_function.__doc__)   # Output: My function's
docstring
```

**2. Keep Decorators Simple:** Decorators should be easy to understand and not overly complex.

```
def simple_decorator(func):
    def wrapper(*args, **kwargs):
        # Simple pre-processing
        result = func(*args, **kwargs)
        # Simple post-processing
        return result
    return wrapper
```

**3. Document Decorators:** Clearly explain what the decorator does, its parameters, and its return type.

```
def logging_decorator(func):
    """Logs the function call details."""
    @wraps(func)
    def wrapper(*args, **kwargs):
        print(f"Calling {func.__name__} with {args} and
{kwargs}")
        result = func(*args, **kwargs)
        print(f"{func.__name__} returned {result}")
        return result
    return wrapper
```

**4. Chain Decorators Carefully:** Be aware of the order in which decorators are applied as it can affect the outcome.

```
@logging_decorator
@simple_decorator
def my_function():
    pass
```

**5. Test Decorators:** Ensure that decorators are tested to verify they work as intended.

```
# Assume we have a decorator 'add_checking'
@add_checking
def add(a, b):
    return a + b

# In your test
assert add(2, 3) == 5
```

**6. Avoid Changing Function Signatures:** Try not to alter the signature of the decorated functions.

```
def decorator(func):
    @wraps(func)
    def wrapper(*args, **kwargs):
        return func(*args, **kwargs)
    return wrapper
```

**7. Use Decorators to Encapsulate Cross-Cutting Concerns:** Use decorators for concerns like logging or authentication, separate from business logic.

```
@authentication_required
def sensitive_operation():
    pass
```

**8. Consider Performance:** Be mindful of the performance impact of decorators, especially in high-traffic functions.

```
import time

def timing_decorator(func):
    @wraps(func)
    def wrapper(*args, **kwargs):
        start_time = time.time()
        result = func(*args, **kwargs)
        end_time = time.time()
        print(f"{func.__name__} took {end_time - start_time}
seconds to run")
        return result
    return wrapper
```

**9. Decorator Factories:** Use a decorator factory when you need to pass arguments to your decorator.

```
def repeat(times):
    def decorator(func):
```

```
        @wraps(func)
        def wrapper(*args, **kwargs):
            for _ in range(times):
                result = func(*args, **kwargs)
            return result
        return wrapper
    return decorator

@repeat(times=3)
def say_hello():
    print("Hello")
```

**10. Avoid Side Effects:** Ensure that decorators don't introduce unintended side effects.

```
def safe_decorator(func):
    @wraps(func)
    def wrapper(*args, **kwargs):
        # Ensure no side effects occur
        return func(*args, **kwargs)
    return wrapper
```

By following these best practices, you can ensure that your use of decorators enhances your code's readability, maintainability, and performance.

# Generators

Generators are a unique feature in Python that allow you to create iterators in a very efficient way. They are particularly useful when you need to iterate over large sets of data without the need to store all of it in memory at once. This is achieved through lazy evaluation, where the next value in the sequence is computed on demand.

## How Generators Work

A generator function is defined like a normal function but uses the `yield` keyword instead of `return`. When called, it returns a generator object but does not start execution immediately. Each time the generator's `__next__()` method is invoked, the generator resumes where it left off, runs until the next `yield` statement, and returns the value after `yield`.

### Advantages of Generators

- **Memory Efficiency**: Since only one item is processed at a time, generators are much more memory-efficient than lists or arrays.
- **Represent Infinite Stream**: Generators can model infinite streams of data.
- **Composable**: Generators can be composed together, allowing you to build complex iterators from simple, understandable pieces.

### Example: Fibonacci Sequence Generator

Here's an example of a generator that produces the Fibonacci sequence:

```
def fibonacci(n):
    a, b = 0, 1
    for _ in range(n):
        yield a
        a, b = b, a + b

# Create a generator for the first 10 Fibonacci numbers
fib_gen = fibonacci(10)

# Iterate through the generator
for num in fib_gen:
    print(num)
```

### Generator Expressions

Similar to list comprehensions, Python also supports generator expressions. They allow you to create a generator without the need for a function.

```
# Generator expression for squares of numbers up to 5
squares = (x**2 for x in range(6))

# Iterate through the generator expression
for square in squares:
    print(square)
```

### Advanced Generator Methods

Generators have methods like `.send()`, `.throw()`, and `.close()` that allow for more complex interactions:

- `.send()` can be used to send a value back to the generator.
- `.throw()` allows you to throw exceptions within the generator.
- `.close()` can be used to stop a generator.

## Use Cases for Data Analysts

Generators can be incredibly useful in various scenarios for data analysis, especially when dealing with large datasets or streams of data. Here are some scenarios where generators can be particularly beneficial:

### Processing Large Datasets

When working with huge datasets that don't fit into memory, you can use generators to load and process data incrementally.

```
def read_large_file(file_name):
    with open(file_name, 'r') as file:
        for line in file:
            yield line.strip()
```

### Data Streaming

Generators are ideal for data streaming applications, such as processing logs in real-time.

```
def follow(logfile):
    logfile.seek(0,2)  # Go to the end of the file
```

```
    while True:
        line = logfile.readline()
        if not line:
            time.sleep(0.1)  # Sleep briefly
            continue
        yield line
```

## Pipeline Processing

You can create a pipeline of data processing steps, where each step is a generator that consumes from the previous one.

```
def process_data(data_stream):
    for data in data_stream:
        # Process the data
        yield processed_data

raw_data = read_large_file('data.log')
processed_data = process_data(raw_data)
```

## Memory-Efficient Iterators

Generators provide a memory-efficient way to iterate over sequences that would be too large to fit in memory.

```
def generate_sequence(n):
    i = 0
    while i < n:
        yield i
        i += 1
```

## Complex Calculations

For complex calculations that need to be performed on-the-fly, generators can calculate and yield results one at a time.

```
def complex_calculation_series():
    result = initial_value
    while True:
        result = complex_calculation(result)
        yield result
```

## Database Querying

When querying databases, generators can fetch and yield rows as needed, which is much more efficient than loading all results at once.

```
def query_database(query):
    for row in database.execute(query):
        yield row
```

These scenarios highlight how generators can be used to handle large data sets efficiently, perform real-time data processing, and create complex data processing pipelines without exhausting system memory.

# Class

## Introduction

In Python, a **class** is like a blueprint for creating objects. An object has properties and behaviors, which in Python are represented by **attributes** and **methods** respectively.

Let's consider a simple `Dog` class to illustrate this:

```
class Dog:
    # Class attribute
    species = "Canis familiaris"

    def __init__(self, name, age):
        # Instance attributes
        self.name = name
        self.age = age

    # Method to return a description
    def description(self):
        return f"{self.name} is {self.age} years old"

    # Method for the dog to speak
    def speak(self, sound):
        return f"{self.name} says {sound}"
```

When we create an instance of the `Dog` class, we can see the output of its methods:

```
# Creating an instance of the Dog class
my_dog = Dog("Rex", 4)

# Output from the description method
print(my_dog.description())  # Output: Rex is 4 years old

# Output from the speak method
print(my_dog.speak("Woof"))  # Output: Rex says Woof
```

Attributes and methods are the fundamental building blocks of Python's class mechanism. They give objects their data and behavior.

# Attributes

Attributes are variables associated with a class. They represent the state or properties of a class and its objects.

- **Class Attributes**: Defined directly within a class and shared by all instances of the class.
- **Instance Attributes**: Defined within methods (usually `__init__`) and unique to each instance.

Here's an example to illustrate:

```
class Dog:
    # Class attribute
    species = "Canis familiaris"

    def __init__(self, name, age):
        # Instance attributes
        self.name = name
        self.age = age
```

In this `Dog` class, `species` is a class attribute, while `name` and `age` are instance attributes.

# Methods

Methods are functions defined inside a class. They describe the behaviors of an object and can modify the object's state.

- **Instance Methods**: Operate on an instance of the class and have access to the instance (`self`) and its attributes.
- **Class Methods**: Operate on the class itself and not on instances. They are marked with the `@classmethod` decorator and take `cls` as the first parameter.
- **Static Methods**: Do not operate on the instance or the class. They are marked with the `@staticmethod` decorator and don't take `self` or `cls` as parameters.

Here's how you define and call methods:

```
class Dog:
    # ...
```

```
    # Instance method
    def description(self):
        return f"{self.name} is {self.age} years old"

    # Another instance method
    def speak(self, sound):
        return f"{self.name} says {sound}"

# Creating an instance of Dog
my_dog = Dog("Rex", 4)

# Calling instance methods
print(my_dog.description())  # Output: Rex is 4 years old
print(my_dog.speak("Woof"))  # Output: Rex says Woof
```

In the `Dog` class, `description` and `speak` are instance methods that act on the `my_dog` instance of the class.

Class methods and static methods are two types of methods that, unlike instance methods, do not require an object of the class to be called.

# Class Methods

A class method is a method that is bound to the class and not the object of the class. It can modify a class state that would apply across all the instances of the class. For defining a class method, you use the `@classmethod` decorator, and it takes `cls` as the first parameter.

```
class Dog:
    # ... previous code

    @classmethod
    def get_species(cls):
        return cls.species
```

You can call a class method using the class name, like so:

```
print(Dog.get_species())  # Output: Canis familiaris
```

# Static Methods

A static method does not take an implicit first argument and is equivalent to a normal function that belongs to a class. It can't access or modify the class state or instance state. You define a static method with the `@staticmethod` decorator.

```
class Dog:
    # ...previous code

    @staticmethod
    def is_dog_friendly():
        return True
```

Static methods can be called using the class name or an instance of the class:

```
print(Dog.is_dog_friendly())  # Output: True
```

Both class methods and static methods are used when you need to perform some operation that isn't unique to any particular instance of the class.

Here are some practical scenarios where class methods and static methods can be implemented in Python:

# Scenario 1: Class Method for Factory Pattern

Imagine you have a `Book` class, and you want to create books with different formats (e.g., paperback, hardcover, ebook). A class method can serve as an alternative constructor.

```
class Book:
    def __init__(self, title, author, format):
        self.title = title
        self.author = author
        self.format = format

    @classmethod
    def paperback(cls, title, author):
        return cls(title, author, 'paperback')

    @classmethod
    def ebook(cls, title, author):
        return cls(title, author, 'ebook')

# Creating different formats of books using class methods
paperback_book = Book.paperback("1984", "George Orwell")
ebook_book = Book.ebook("Brave New World", "Aldous Huxley")
```

## Scenario 2: Static Method for Validation

Suppose you have a `User` class, and you need to validate email addresses before creating a user instance. A static method is perfect for this.

```
class User:
    def __init__(self, username, email):
        self.username = username
        self.email = email

    @staticmethod
    def is_valid_email(email_addr):
        return '@' in email_addr

# Validating an email before creating a User instance
if User.is_valid_email("test@example.com"):
    user = User("testuser", "test@example.com")
```

## Scenario 3: Class Method for Maintaining State

Let's say you have a `Logger` class that keeps track of the number of log messages. A class method can be used to update this state across all instances.

```
class Logger:
    count = 0

    def __init__(self, name):
        self.name = name

    @classmethod
    def log(cls, message):
        print(f"Log message: {message}")
        cls.count += 1

# Logging messages and updating the count
Logger.log("System started")
Logger.log("An error occurred")
```

In these scenarios, class methods and static methods fulfill specific roles that instance methods cannot, such as creating instances in a controlled manner, performing utility tasks, and maintaining a state that is shared across all instances.

Here are some scenarios where class methods and static methods can be applied in the context of data analysis:

## Scenario 1: Class Method for Data Aggregation

Imagine you have a `DataAnalyzer` class that processes various datasets. A class method can be used to aggregate data from multiple instances of the class.

```
class DataAnalyzer:
    data_count = 0

    def __init__(self, data):
        self.data = data
        DataAnalyzer.data_count += len(data)

    @classmethod
    def total_data_points(cls):
        return cls.data_count

# Aggregating data points from multiple datasets
dataset1 = DataAnalyzer([1, 2, 3])
dataset2 = DataAnalyzer([4, 5, 6, 7])
print(DataAnalyzer.total_data_points())  # Output: 7
```

## Scenario 2: Static Method for Data Validation

Suppose you have a `Dataset` class, and you need to ensure that the data passed to it is of the correct type. A static method can be used for this validation.

```
class Dataset:
    def __init__(self, data):
        self.data = data

    @staticmethod
    def validate(data):
        return isinstance(data, list)

# Validating the data before creating a Dataset instance
data = [1, 2, 3]
if Dataset.validate(data):
    dataset = Dataset(data)
```

## Scenario 3: Class Method for Data Transformation

Let's say you have a `TimeSeriesData` class that handles time-series data. You can use a class method to apply a transformation to all instances of the class.

```
class TimeSeriesData:
    def __init__(self, timestamps, values):
        self.timestamps = timestamps
        self.values = values

    @classmethod
    def from_csv(cls, csv_file):
        # Assume we have a function to read CSV files and
return timestamps and values
        timestamps, values = read_csv(csv_file)
        return cls(timestamps, values)

# Creating a TimeSeriesData instance from a CSV file
time_series_data = TimeSeriesData.from_csv('data.csv')
```

# Inheritance

Inheritance allows us to define a class that inherits all the methods and properties from another class. This is particularly useful in data analysis for creating specialized classes based on a general template.

**Base Class:** `DataFrame`

Imagine a base class called `DataFrame` that represents a generic dataset:

```
class DataFrame:
    def __init__(self, data):
        self.data = data

    def summary(self):
        # Returns a summary of the data
        pass
```

**Derived Class:** `TimeSeriesDataFrame`

Now, we create a derived class that extends `DataFrame` to handle time-series data specifically:

```
class TimeSeriesDataFrame(DataFrame):
    def __init__(self, data, timestamps):
        super().__init__(data)
        self.timestamps = timestamps

    def time_summary(self):
        # Returns a time-series specific summary
        pass
```

In this scenario, `TimeSeriesDataFrame` inherits from `DataFrame`, allowing it to use the `summary` method and adding a new method `time_summary` for time-series-specific analysis.

**Single Inheritance**

Single inheritance occurs when a class inherits from one parent class. This is the most common use of inheritance.

```
class BaseDataModel:
    def __init__(self, data):
        self.data = data

    def clean_data(self):
        # Code to clean data
        pass

class TimeSeriesModel(BaseDataModel):
    def __init__(self, data, sequence):
        super().__init__(data)
        self.sequence = sequence

    def time_series_analysis(self):
        # Code for time series analysis
        pass
```

In this example, `TimeSeriesModel` inherits from `BaseDataModel`, gaining access to its methods and attributes.

**Multiple Inheritance**

Multiple inheritance occurs when a class can inherit attributes and methods from more than one parent class.

```
class SpatialModel:
    def spatial_analysis(self):
        # Code for spatial analysis
        pass
```

```
class SpatioTemporalModel(TimeSeriesModel, SpatialModel):
    def __init__(self, data, sequence, coordinates):
        TimeSeriesModel.__init__(self, data, sequence)
        SpatialModel.__init__(self)
        self.coordinates = coordinates

    def combined_analysis(self):
        # Code that utilizes both time series and spatial
analysis
        pass
```

Here, `SpatioTemporalModel` inherits from both `TimeSeriesModel` and `SpatialModel`, combining their functionalities.

**Method Resolution Order (MRO)**

Method Resolution Order is the order in which Python looks for a method in a hierarchy of classes. It becomes especially important in multiple inheritance as it determines which method will be executed.

```
print(SpatioTemporalModel.mro())
```

This will print the order in which methods are resolved.

**Mixins**

Mixins are a sort of multiple inheritance where the inherited classes provide methods that enhance the functionality of the base class.

```
class DataMixin:
    def export_data(self, format):
        # Code to export data in various formats
        pass

class CustomModel(BaseDataModel, DataMixin):
    pass
```

`CustomModel` now has an additional method `export_data` from `DataMixin`.

**Abstract Base Classes (ABCs)**

Abstract Base Classes are classes that are only meant to be inherited from; you cannot create instances of an ABC. They allow you to define methods that must be created within any child classes built from the ABC.

```
from abc import ABC, abstractmethod

class AbstractDataModel(ABC):
    @abstractmethod
    def save(self):
        pass

class ConcreteDataModel(AbstractDataModel):
    def save(self):
        # Implementation of save method
        pass
```

Here, `ConcreteDataModel` provides an implementation of the `save` method defined in `AbstractDataModel`.

**Interface Inheritance**

In Python, interface inheritance is not enforced like in some other languages. However, we can create classes that define a set of methods that must be implemented by any non-abstract child class. This is more of a convention in Python.

```
class DataProcessorInterface:
    def load_data(self):
        raise NotImplementedError

    def process_data(self):
        raise NotImplementedError

class CSVDataProcessor(DataProcessorInterface):
    def load_data(self):
        # Implementation for loading CSV data
        pass

    def process_data(self):
        # Implementation for processing CSV data
        pass
```

Here, `CSVDataProcessor` implements the interface defined by `DataProcessorInterface`.

**Composition Over Inheritance**

Sometimes, it's better to use composition rather than inheritance. Composition involves including instances of other classes as attributes, rather than inheriting from them.

```
class DataLoader:
    def load_data(self, source):
        # Code to load data from the source
        pass

class DataAnalyzer:
    def __init__(self, loader):
        self.loader = loader

    def analyze(self):
        data = self.loader.load_data()
        # Code to analyze data
        pass

# Using composition
loader = DataLoader()
analyzer = DataAnalyzer(loader)
```

In this example, `DataAnalyzer` is composed of `DataLoader`, allowing it to use `DataLoader`'s `load_data` method.

### Dependency Injection

Dependency injection is a technique where an object supplies the dependencies of another object. This can be used to change the behavior of a class without altering the class itself.

```
class DataVisualizer:
    def __init__(self, plotter):
        self.plotter = plotter

    def visualize(self, data):
        self.plotter.plot(data)

class MatplotlibPlotter:
    def plot(self, data):
        # Code to plot data using Matplotlib
        pass

# Injecting the dependency
plotter = MatplotlibPlotter()
visualizer = DataVisualizer(plotter)
```

Here, `DataVisualizer` does not need to know the details of how `MatplotlibPlotter` works, just that it has a `plot` method.

# Polymorphism

Polymorphism allows us to define methods in the child class with the same name as defined in their parent class. This is useful when we want to modify or extend the behavior of base class methods.

### Overriding Methods

Let's say we want to override the `summary` method in our `TimeSeriesDataFrame` to provide more detailed analysis:

```
class TimeSeriesDataFrame(DataFrame):
    # ... previous code

    def summary(self):
        # Overridden method to provide a detailed time-series
summary
        pass
```

With polymorphism, the `summary` method behaves differently depending on whether it's called on a `DataFrame` object or a `TimeSeriesDataFrame` object.

### Method Overriding

Method overriding is a feature of inheritance that allows a subclass to provide a specific implementation of a method that is already defined in its superclass.

```
class DataModel:
    def save(self):
        print("DataModel save method.")

class CSVDataModel(DataModel):
    def save(self):
        print("CSVDataModel save method, saving data in CSV
format.")
```

Here, `CSVDataModel` overrides the `save` method of `DataModel`. When you call `save` on an object of `CSVDataModel`, it will use the overridden method.

### Duck Typing

Duck typing is a concept related to polymorphism where the type or class of an object is less important than the methods it defines. If an object "quacks like a duck and walks like a duck," then it can be used as if it is a duck.

```
class PandasDataModel:
    def plot(self):
        print("Plotting with pandas.")

class MatplotlibDataModel:
    def plot(self):
        print("Plotting with matplotlib.")

def plot_data(model):
    model.plot()

pandas_model = PandasDataModel()
matplotlib_model = MatplotlibDataModel()

plot_data(pandas_model)  # Output: Plotting with pandas.
plot_data(matplotlib_model)  # Output: Plotting with
matplotlib.
```

In this example, `plot_data` function can accept any object that has a `plot` method, regardless of its class.

**Operator Overloading**

Operator overloading allows objects to interact with arithmetic or logical operators. For example, you can define how the + operator should work with objects of a custom class.

```
class DataPoint:
    def __init__(self, value):
        self.value = value

    def __add__(self, other):
        return DataPoint(self.value + other.value)

point1 = DataPoint(10)
point2 = DataPoint(20)
result = point1 + point2
print(result.value)  # Output: 30
```

Here, the + operator is overloaded to add the values of two `DataPoint` instances.

**Function and Method Arguments**

Polymorphism is also useful when you want to write functions or methods that can accept many types of objects.

Consider a scenario where we have different data visualizations that we want to render. We might have bar charts, line charts, and scatter plots, but we want to treat them all as generic "plots" that we can render.

```
class Plot:
    def render(self):
        raise NotImplementedError("Subclass must implement
abstract method")

class BarChart(Plot):
    def render(self):
        return "Rendering Bar Chart"

class LineChart(Plot):
    def render(self):
        return "Rendering Line Chart"

class ScatterPlot(Plot):
    def render(self):
        return "Rendering Scatter Plot"

def render_plot(plot):
    print(plot.render())

# Using polymorphism to render different plot types
plots = [BarChart(), LineChart(), ScatterPlot()]
for plot in plots:
    render_plot(plot)
```

In this example, each subclass of `Plot` implements the `render` method differently. The `render_plot` function can call `render` on any `Plot` object, regardless of its actual class, and the correct method is called.

**Abstract Classes and Interfaces**

Python's `abc` module allows us to define abstract base classes and interfaces, which can enforce certain methods to be implemented by subclasses.

```
from abc import ABC, abstractmethod

class DataAnalyzer(ABC):
    @abstractmethod
```

```
    def analyze(self):
        pass

class PandasDataAnalyzer(DataAnalyzer):
    def analyze(self):
        return "Analyzing data using pandas"

class NumpyDataAnalyzer(DataAnalyzer):
    def analyze(self):
        return "Analyzing data using numpy"
```

Subclasses of `DataAnalyzer` must implement the `analyze` method, ensuring that they can be used polymorphically.

# Encapsulation

Encapsulation is the bundling of data with the methods that operate on that data. It restricts direct access to some of an object's components, which is useful for preventing accidental modification of data.

In Python, encapsulation is achieved through the use of private and protected members, which are attributes or methods that should not be accessed directly from outside the class.

- **Private members** are denoted by two underscores __ at the beginning of their names. They cannot be accessed directly from outside the class but can be accessed within the class.
- **Protected members** are denoted by a single underscore _ at the beginning of their names. They are intended to be used only within the class and its subclasses.

```
class Account:
    def __init__(self):
        self._balance = 0  # Protected attribute
        self.__account_number = 123456789  # Private 
attribute

    def deposit(self, amount):
        if amount > 0:
            self._balance += amount
            self.__update_ledger(amount)

    def __update_ledger(self, amount):
        # Private method to update the ledger
```

```
        pass
```

In this Account class, _balance is a protected attribute, and __account_number and __update_ledger are private members.

## Getter and Setter Methods

Encapsulation also involves the use of getter and setter methods (also known as accessors and mutators). These methods allow you to control how attributes are accessed and modified.

```
class Account:
    # ... previous code

    def get_balance(self):
        # Getter method for _balance
        return self._balance

    def set_balance(self, value):
        # Setter method for _balance
        if value >= 0:
            self._balance = value
```

Here, get_balance and set_balance are used to access and modify the _balance attribute safely.

## Benefits of Encapsulation

- **Control**: Encapsulation gives control over the data by restricting what can be done with it.
- **Flexibility**: You can change the internal implementation of the class without affecting the classes that use it.
- **Maintenance**: It makes the code more maintainable and understandable.
- **Security**: It prevents the object's state from being corrupted by external processes.

Encapsulation not only serves to keep the data within an object secure from outside interference, but it also plays a crucial role in the concept of data hiding in object-oriented programming. By restricting direct access to some of an object's components, encapsulation ensures that the object can be used with no need to understand its internal complexities. This abstraction layer makes the use of complex objects manageable in larger software systems.

## A Closer Look

Python's approach to encapsulation is often considered "gentleman's encapsulation" because it's based on a convention rather than strict enforcement. The language's philosophy is "we are all consenting adults here," meaning that while you can access private members, adhere to the convention and respect the intended level of access.

```
class Example:
    def __init__(self):
        self._semi_private = "Accessible, but please don't"
        self.__private = "This is really meant to be private"

    def _semi_private_method(self):
        # This method is semi-private and should be treated
as part of the internal API.
        pass

    def __private_method(self):
        # This method is truly intended to be private and not
accessible from outside.
        pass
```

In this `Example` class, `_semi_private` and `_semi_private_method` are protected members, while `__private` and `__private_method` are private. The double underscore will cause name mangling, which makes it harder (but not impossible) to access from outside the class.

Name mangling is a mechanism used in Python to prevent name clashes in subclasses. It's a way to ensure that private variables and methods in a class cannot be easily accessed from outside the class, including from its subclasses.

Here's how name mangling works:

- When you prefix an attribute name with two underscores __, Python internally changes the name of the attribute to `_ClassName__attributeName`.
- This is done to prevent the attribute from being overridden in subclasses.
- The mangled name is accessible within the class methods but not easily from outside.

Let's look at an example:

```
class Parent:
    def __init__(self):
        self.__private = "I'm private!"

    def _get_private(self):
        return self.__private

class Child(Parent):
    def __init__(self):
        super().__init__()
        self.__private = "I'm a different private!"


child = Child()

# This will print "I'm private!" because the name mangling
protects the private variable in the parent class.
print(child._get_private())

# This will raise an AttributeError because __private is
name-mangled and not directly accessible.
print(child.__private)
```

In the `Child` class, `__private` is a different attribute from `__private` in the `Parent` class because of name mangling. The `Child` class has its own mangled version of `__private`.

Name mangling is Python's way to achieve a stronger level of protection for attributes, making them private in a sense. However, it's still possible to access these attributes if you know the mangled name, which is why it's sometimes referred to as "weak" private.

## Accessing Mangled Names

Despite the name mangling, it's still possible to access these "private" attributes from outside the class if you know the pattern Python uses to mangle the names:

```
instance = Child()
print(instance._Child__private)  # This will work and print
"I'm private

print(child._Parent__private)  # This will work and print
"I'm a different private!
```

However, this is strongly discouraged, as it goes against the intent of encapsulation.

Here are a few scenarios that illustrate the use of encapsulation:

**Scenario 1: Bank Account Management**

```
class BankAccount:
    def __init__(self, initial_balance):
        self.__balance = initial_balance  # Private attribute

    def deposit(self, amount):
        if amount > 0:
            self.__balance += amount
            self.__update_transaction_history(amount, 
"deposit")

    def withdraw(self, amount):
        if 0 < amount <= self.__balance:
            self.__balance -= amount
            self.__update_transaction_history(amount, 
"withdrawal")

    def get_balance(self):
        return self.__balance

    def __update_transaction_history(self, amount, 
transaction_type):
        # Private method to update transaction history
        pass
```

In this scenario, a `BankAccount` class encapsulates the balance and transaction history. The balance is a private attribute, preventing direct access from outside the class. Public methods like `deposit`, `withdraw`, and `get_balance` provide controlled access to the balance.

**Scenario 2: Data Analysis Toolkit**

```
class DataAnalyzer:
    def __init__(self, data):
        self.__data = data  # Private attribute

    def analyze(self):
        # Public method to analyze data
        results = self.__perform_complex_analysis()
        return results
```

```
    def __perform_complex_analysis(self):
        # Private method with complex data analysis logic
        pass
```

Here, a `DataAnalyzer` class encapsulates the data and the complex analysis logic within private methods. Users of the class can call the `analyze` method to get the analysis results with no need to understand the underlying complex algorithms.

**Scenario 3: Employee Management System**

```
class Employee:
    def __init__(self, name, salary):
        self.__name = name  # Private attribute
        self.__salary = salary  # Private attribute

    def get_salary(self):
        # Public method to safely access the employee's
salary
        return self.__salary

    def __calculate_tax(self):
        # Private method to calculate tax based on salary
        pass

    def report_finances(self):
        tax = self.__calculate_tax()
        net_salary = self.__salary - tax
        return {"gross_salary": self.__salary, "tax": tax,
"net_salary": net_salary}
```

In this example, the `Employee` class encapsulates the name and salary of an employee. It provides public methods to access the salary and report finances, while the calculation of taxes is kept private within the class.

# Composition

Composition is a design principle where a class comprises one or more objects from other classes. It allows for creating complex types by combining objects of other types, implying a relationship where the composed object cannot exist independently of its parent.

## Defining Composition

- Composition is often defined as a "has-a" relationship.
- It is a more flexible and less tightly coupled arrangement than inheritance.
- It allows for components to be easily replaced or changed.

## Example of Composition

```
class Engine:
    def start(self):
        pass

    def stop(self):
        pass

class Car:
    def __init__(self):
        self.engine = Engine()  # Composition: Car "has an"
Engine

    def start(self):
        self.engine.start()

    def stop(self):
        self.engine.stop()
```

In this example, `Car` is composed of `Engine`. The `Car` class doesn't inherit the `Engine` class but rather holds an instance of it.

## Benefits of Composition

- **Reusability**: Objects can be reused across different classes.
- **Flexibility**: It's easy to change the behavior at runtime by changing the composed object.
- **Maintainability**: Changes in the composed classes do not affect the parent class.

Composition provides an alternative to inheritance for building complex objects and is a key technique in creating a flexible and maintainable codebase. It's particularly useful when objects need to be composed of several other objects with complex interactions.

# Aggregation

Aggregation is a specialized form of association that represents a "whole-part" relationship between the aggregate (whole) and a component part. This means that while the part can belong to one aggregate, it is not exclusively tied to that aggregate.

## Defining Aggregation

- Aggregation is characterized by a "has-a" relationship but differs from composition in that the lifetime of the 'part' is not managed by the lifetime of the 'whole'.
- The 'part' (component) can exist independently of the 'whole' (aggregate).

## Example of Aggregation

```
class Classroom:
    def __init__(self):
        self.students = []

    def add_student(self, student):
        self.students.append(student)

class Student:
    def __init__(self, name):
        self.name = name

# Aggregation relationship
classroom = Classroom()
student = Student("Alice")
classroom.add_student(student)
```

In this example, `Classroom` aggregates `Student` objects. Students can exist without a classroom, and they can also be part of multiple classrooms.

## Benefits of Aggregation

- **Flexibility**: It allows for the representation of complex relationships where components can be shared and interact in various ways.
- **Reusability**: Components can be reused in different contexts.
- **Loose Coupling**: Changes to the component class do not affect the

aggregate class.

Aggregation provides a way to build flexible systems that can model real-world relationships where components have their own lifecycle and can be part of multiple aggregates.

# Special Methods

Special methods in Python, also known as magic methods or dunder methods (because they have double underscores at the beginning and end of their names), are a set of predefined methods that you can use to enrich your classes. They are the means by which you can define the behavior of objects in relation to Python's built-in language constructs.

Here's an overview of some commonly used special methods:

## `__init__(self, ...)`

This method is called when an instance of the class is created. It's used for initializing the attributes of the class.

```
class Example:
    def __init__(self, value):
        self.value = value
```

## `__str__(self)`

This method returns the string representation of the object, which is called by the `str(object)` built-in function and by the `print` function.

```
class Example:
    # ... previous code
    def __str__(self):
        return f"Example with value: {self.value}"
```

## `__repr__(self)`

This method returns an unambiguous string representation of the object, which could recreate the object. It's called by the `repr()` built-in function.

```
class Example:
    # ... previous code
    def __repr__(self):
        return f"Example({self.value})"
```

## `__eq__(self, other)`

Defines behavior for the equality operator, ==.

```
class Example:
    # ... previous code
    def __eq__(self, other):
        if isinstance(other, Example):
            return self.value == other.value
        return False
```

## `__add__(self, other)`

Defines behavior for the addition operator, +.

```
class Example:
    # ... previous code
    def __add__(self, other):
        if isinstance(other, Example):
            return Example(self.value + other.value)
        return NotImplemented
```

## `__iter__(self)` and `__next__(self)`

These methods are used to make an object iterable.

```
class Example:
    def __init__(self, data):
        self.data = data
        self.index = 0

    def __iter__(self):
        return self

    def __next__(self):
        if self.index >= len(self.data):
            raise StopIteration
        result = self.data[self.index]
        self.index += 1
        return result
```

## `__getitem__(self, key)`

Defines behavior for accessing an item using indexing or slicing.

```
class Example:
    # ... previous code
```

```
    def __getitem__(self, key):
        return self.data[key]
```

## `__enter__(self)` and `__exit__(self, exc_type, exc_value, traceback)`

These methods define what the object does at the beginning and the end of a `with` block.

```
class Example:
    def __enter__(self):
        print("Enter the context")
        return self

    def __exit__(self, exc_type, exc_value, traceback):
        print("Exit the context")
```

Special methods allow you to emulate the behavior of built-in types and implement an interface that's familiar to Python users. They are a powerful feature that enables elegant and intuitive object-oriented designs.

# @property

The `@property` decorator in Python is a built-in decorator that allows you to use class methods as attributes, which can be very useful when you want to implement attributes that are accessed and modified through getter and setter methods. This is a part of the encapsulation concept, where you want to hide the internal representation of the attribute and only expose a public interface.

Here's a deeper look into how `@property` works:

### Using `@property` for Getter

The @property decorator turns a method into a "getter" for a property:

```
class Celsius:
    def __init__(self, temperature=0):
        self._temperature = temperature

    @property
    def temperature(self):
        print("Getting value...")
        return self._temperature
```

In this example, temperature can be accessed like a regular attribute, but when accessed, the temperature method is called, which prints "Getting value..." and then returns the internal _temperature value.

## Using `@property` for Setter

To set the value of a property, you can define a setter method using the `@property_name.setter` decorator:

```
class Celsius:
    # ... previous code

    @temperature.setter
    def temperature(self, value):
        if value < -273.15:
            raise ValueError("Temperature below -273.15 is
not possible.")
        print("Setting value...")
        self._temperature = value
```

Now, when you assign a value to `temperature`, the `temperature` setter method is called, which validates the new value before setting it.

## Using `@property` for Deleter

You can also define a deleter method that is invoked when you delete the property:

```
class Celsius:
    # ... previous code

    @temperature.deleter
    def temperature(self):
        print("Deleting value...")
        del self._temperature
```

With the deleter, calling `del object.temperature` will invoke the `temperature` deleter method.

## Advantages of Using `@property`

- **Encapsulation**: It allows you to encapsulate attribute access and ensure that certain constraints or conditions are met.
- **Validation**: You can add validation logic to the setter to check for valid

values.

- **Computed Properties**: You can use getters to compute a value rather than just returning it.

The `@property` decorator is a powerful feature that allows for cleaner and more maintainable code by ensuring that data encapsulation is respected.

Class decorators in Python are a powerful feature that allow you to modify or enhance the behavior of classes in a reusable and elegant way. They are similar to function decorators, but they are applied to classes instead of functions.

Here's a deeper look into class decorators:

## Understanding Class Decorators

A class decorator is a function that takes a class as an argument and returns either the same class or a new class that has been somehow enhanced.

```
def my_class_decorator(cls):
    # Do something with the class
    return cls
```

You apply a class decorator above the class definition using the @ syntax.

```
@my_class_decorator
class MyClass:
    pass
```

## Common Uses of Class Decorators

- **Adding Class Attributes**: You can add new attributes to the class.
- **Modifying Method Behavior**: You can wrap or replace methods of the class to change their behavior.
- **Registering Classes**: You can automatically register classes in some registry, which is useful for things like plugins.
- **Singleton Pattern**: You can ensure a class only has one instance.

## Example: Adding a Class Attribute

Here's an example of a class decorator that adds a new attribute to a class:

```
def add_attribute(attribute_name, value):
```

```
    def decorator(cls):
        setattr(cls, attribute_name, value)
        return cls
    return decorator

@add_attribute('greeting', 'Hello, World!')
class MyClass:
    pass

print(MyClass.greeting)  # Output: Hello, World!
```

## Example: Singleton Pattern

A singleton is a design pattern that restricts a class to a single instance. Here's how you might implement a singleton using a class decorator:

```
def singleton(cls):
    instances = {}
    def get_instance(*args, **kwargs):
        if cls not in instances:
            instances[cls] = cls(*args, **kwargs)
        return instances[cls]
    return get_instance

@singleton
class Database:
    pass

db1 = Database()
db2 = Database()
print(db1 is db2)  # Output: True
```

In this example, the `singleton` decorator ensures that only one instance of `Database` is created, no matter how many times it is instantiated.

## Best Practices

- **Keep Decorators Simple**: Decorators should be simple to understand and maintain.
- **Use Wraps**: When writing decorators, use `functools.wraps` to preserve the original class's information.
- **Document Decorators**: Clearly document what the decorator does and how it modifies the class behavior.

Class decorators are a powerful tool for abstracting away repetitive code and adding functionality to classes in a DRY (Don't Repeat Yourself) manner.

# Metaclasses

Metaclasses in Python are a deep and advanced topic that touches on the very essence of how classes are constructed. They are sometimes referred to as "classes of classes" because they define the behavior and rules of class objects themselves.

Here's a deeper look into metaclasses:

### What Are Metaclasses?

- A metaclass in Python is a class of a class that defines how a class behaves. A class is an instance of a metaclass.
- A metaclass can be thought of as the "type" of a class, just as a class is the "type" of an instance.

### The Default Metaclass: `type`

- In Python, the default metaclass is `type`. You can use `type` to dynamically create classes.
- `type` can take the name of the class, a tuple of base classes, and a dictionary containing attributes and methods.

```
MyKlass = type('MyKlass', (BaseClass,), {'x': 10, 'y': 20})
```

### Custom Metaclasses

- You can create custom metaclasses by inheriting from `type` and overriding `__new__` or `__init__`.
- Custom metaclasses can be used to modify class creation, for example, to enforce certain attributes or methods, or to automatically register classes.

```
class Meta(type):
    def __new__(cls, name, bases, dct):
        # Custom logic for class creation
        return super().__new__(cls, name, bases, dct)

class MyClass(metaclass=Meta):
    pass
```

## Using Metaclasses

- Metaclasses are used in frameworks like Django to do things like creating models from simple class definitions.
- They can be used to implement design patterns like Singleton by ensuring a class only ever has one instance.

## Why Use Metaclasses?

- **Control and Customization**: Metaclasses allow you to control the creation of classes and customize class behavior in ways that can't be done with class decorators or other mechanisms.
- **Framework Development**: They are a powerful tool for framework developers who need to create APIs that allow users to define behavior in a declarative way.

## Caution with Metaclasses

- Metaclasses can make code more complex and harder to understand.
- They should be used sparingly and only when there is a clear benefit that cannot be achieved through simpler means.

Metaclasses are a deep part of Python's OOP system and provide a level of control over classes that is not possible with other tools. They are a powerful feature, but with great power comes great responsibility. It's important to use them wisely and document their use well.

# Reading and Writing Files

Text files are one of the most common types of data sources you will encounter as a Python programmer. They can store plain text, such as a novel or a poem, or structured text, such as a CSV file or a JSON file. In this chapter, you will learn how to read and write text files in Python using various techniques and methods.

## Reading Data from a Text File

To read data from a text file, you need to open the file using the built-in `open()` function. This function returns a file object you can use to access the file's contents. The `open()` function takes two arguments: the name of the file and the mode of operation. The mode can be either `'r'` for reading, `'w'` for writing, `'a'` for appending, or `'r+'` for both reading and writing. For example, to open a file named `data.txt` for reading, you can write:

```
file = open('data.txt', 'r')
```

Once you have opened the file, you can use various methods to read its data. The most common methods are:

- `read()`: This method reads the entire file and returns a string containing the file's contents. For example, to read the whole file and print it, you can write:

```
file = open('data.txt', 'r')
data = file.read()
print(data)
file.close()
```

Note that you should always close the file after you are done with it using the `close()` method. This will free up the resources used by the file and prevent any errors or data loss.

- `readline()`: This method reads one line from the file and returns a string containing the line. You can use this method in a loop to read the file line by line. For example, to read the file and print each line, you can write:

```
file = open('data.txt', 'r')
```

```
line = file.readline()
while line != '':
    print(line)
    line = file.readline()
file.close()
```

Note that each line returned by `readline()` includes the newline character (`'\n'`) at the end. You can use the `strip()` method to remove any leading or trailing whitespace from the line.

- `readlines()`: This method reads all the lines from the file and returns a list of strings, each containing one line. You can use this method to store the file's contents in a list and process them later. For example, to read the file and store each line in a list, you can write:

```
file = open('data.txt', 'r')
lines = file.readlines()
file.close()
```

You can then access each line in the list using indexing or looping. For example, to print the first line in the list, you can write:

```
print(lines[0])
```

# Writing Data to a Text File

To write data to a text file, you need to open the file using the `open()` function with the mode `'w'` for writing. This will create a new file if it does not exist, or overwrite the existing file if it does. For example, to open a file named `output.txt` for writing, you can write:

```
file = open('output.txt', 'w')
```

Once you have opened the file, you can use various methods to write data to it. The most common methods are:

- `write()`: This method writes a string to the file. You can use this method to write any data that can be converted to a string, such as numbers, booleans, or lists. For example, to write the string `'Hello, world!'` to the file, you can write:

```
file = open('output.txt', 'w')
file.write('Hello, world!')
```

```
file.close()
```

Note that the `write()` method does not add a newline character (`'\n'`) at the end of the string. If you want to write multiple lines to the file, you need to add the newline character yourself. For example, to write two lines to the file, you can write:

```
file = open('output.txt', 'w')
file.write('Hello, world!\n')
file.write('This is a new line.\n')
file.close()
```

- `writelines()`: This method writes a list of strings to the file. Each string in the list is written as a separate line. You can use this method to write a list of data to the file in one go. For example, to write a list of numbers to the file, you can write:

```
file = open('output.txt', 'w')
numbers = [1, 2, 3, 4, 5]
file.writelines([str(n) + '\n' for n in numbers])
file.close()
```

Note that the `writelines()` method does not add a newline character (`'\n'`) at the end of each string in the list. You need to add the newline character yourself, as shown in the example.

## Appending Data to an Existing File

To append data to an existing file, you need to open the file using the `open()` function with the mode `'a'` for appending. This will open the file and move the file pointer to the end of the file, so that any data you write will be added to the file without overwriting its contents. For example, to open a file named `output.txt` for appending, you can write:

```
file = open('output.txt', 'a')
```

Once you have opened the file, you can use the same methods as writing to write data to the file. For example, to append the string `'This is an appended line.\n'` to the file, you can write:

```
file = open('output.txt', 'a')
file.write('This is an appended line.\n')
file.close()
```

## Handling Different File Encodings and Character Sets

When you open a file for reading or writing, you need to specify the encoding of the file, which is the way the file's contents are represented as bytes. The default encoding in Python is UTF-8, which is a universal encoding that can handle any character set. However, some files may use different encodings, such as ASCII, Latin-1, or Windows-1252, which may not be compatible with UTF-8. If you try to read or write a file with a different encoding, you may encounter errors or data corruption.

To avoid this, you need to specify the encoding of the file when you open it using the `open()` function. You can use the `encoding` argument to provide the name of the encoding, such as `'ascii'`, `'latin-1'`, or `'windows-1252'`. For example, to open a file named `data.txt` with the encoding `'latin-1'`, you can write:

```
file = open('data.txt', 'r', encoding='latin-1')
```

You can also use the `errors` argument to specify how to handle any encoding errors that may occur. The default value is `'strict'`, which means that any encoding error will raise an exception. You can use other values, such as `'ignore'`, `'replace'`, or `'backslashreplace'`, to ignore, replace, or escape the invalid characters. For example, to open a file named `data.txt` with the encoding `'latin-1'` and replace any invalid characters with `'?'`, you can write:

```
file = open('data.txt', 'r', encoding='latin-1',
errors='replace')
```

## Handling Different Delimiters or Separators in Data Files

Some text files may contain structured data, such as tables, records, or matrices, that are separated by delimiters or separators. A delimiter or separator is a character or a sequence of characters that marks the boundary between different data elements. The most common delimiter is the comma (`,`), which is used in CSV (comma-separated values) files. However, some files may use other delimiters, such as tabs (`\t`), spaces (` `), semicolons (`;`), or colons (`:`).

To read or write data from or to a file with a different delimiter, you need to specify the delimiter when you open the file using the `open()` function. You can use the `delimiter` argument to provide the character or the sequence of characters that separates the data elements. For example, to open a file named `data.txt` with the delimiter `';'`, you can write:

```
file = open('data.txt', 'r', delimiter=';')
```

Once you have opened the file, you can use the same methods as reading or writing to access the data. However, each line or string that you read or write will contain the delimiter, so you need to split or join the data elements accordingly. For example, to read the file and print each data element, you can write:

```
file = open('data.txt', 'r', delimiter=';')
line = file.readline()
while line != '':
    elements = line.split(';')
    for element in elements:
        print(element)
    line = file.readline()
file.close()
```

Note that the `split()` method returns a list of strings that are separated by the delimiter. You can use the `join()` method to join a list of strings with a delimiter. For example, to write a list of numbers to the file with the delimiter `';'`, you can write:

```
file = open('output.txt', 'w', delimiter=';')
numbers = [6, 7, 8, 9, 10]
file.writelines([';'.join([str(n) for n in numbers]) + '\n'])
file.close()
```

# Handling Data Errors, Exceptions, and Validation

When you read or write data from or to a file, you may encounter various errors or exceptions that can interrupt or corrupt the data processing. Some common errors or exceptions are:

- `FileNotFoundError`: This exception is raised when you try to open a file that does not exist or that you do not have permission to access. To avoid this, you should check if the file exists and if you have the right permissions before opening it. You can use the `os.path.exists()` function to check if the file exists, and the `os.access()` function to check if you have the permission to read or write the file. For example, to check if the file named `data.txt` exists and if you can read it, you can write:

```
import os
if os.path.exists('data.txt') and os.access('data.txt',
os.R_OK):
    file = open('data.txt', 'r')
else:
    print('File does not exist or cannot be read.')
```

- `PermissionError`: This exception is raised when you try to open a file that you do not have permission to access or modify. To avoid this, you should check if you have the right permissions before opening the file, as shown in the previous example. You can also use the `os.chmod()` function to change the permissions of the file, if you have the authority to do so. For example, to change the permissions of the file named `data.txt` to allow reading and writing by the owner, you can write:

```
import os
os.chmod('data.txt', 0o600)
file = open('data.txt', 'r+')
```

- `ValueError`: This exception is raised when you try to perform an operation on the file that is incompatible with the mode of the file. For example, if you try to write to a file that is opened for reading, or read from a file that is opened for writing, you will get a `ValueError`. To avoid this, you should make sure that you open the file with the correct mode for the operation that you want to perform. For example, to write to a file named `output.txt`, you should open it with the mode `'w'` or `'a'`, not `'r'` or `'r+'`. You can write:

```
file = open('output.txt', 'w')
file.write('This is a valid operation.\n')
file.close()
```

- `UnicodeDecodeError`: This exception is raised when you try to read a file with an encoding that does not match the encoding of the file. For example, if you try to read a file that is encoded in Latin-1 with the default encoding UTF-8, you will get a `UnicodeDecodeError`. To avoid this, you should specify the encoding of the file when you open it using the `open()` function, as shown in the previous section. For example, to read a file named `data.txt` that is encoded in Latin-1, you should open it with the encoding `'latin-1'`. You can write:

```
file = open('data.txt', 'r', encoding='latin-1')
data = file.read()
print(data)
file.close()
```

- `UnicodeEncodeError`: This exception is raised when you try to write a file with an encoding that does not support the characters that you want to write. For example, if you try to write a file that is encoded in ASCII with some non-ASCII characters, such as accented letters or symbols, you will get a `UnicodeEncodeError`. To avoid this, you should specify the encoding of the file when you open it using the `open()` function, and use an encoding that can handle the characters that you want to write. For example, to write a file named `output.txt` that contains some non-ASCII characters, you should open it with the encoding `'utf-8'`. You can write:

```
file = open('output.txt', 'w', encoding='utf-8')
file.write('This is a valid operation with non-ASCII
characters: é, ñ, €.\n')
file.close()
```

In addition to handling errors and exceptions, you should also validate and clean the data that you read from or write to a file. Validation means checking if the data meets certain criteria or rules, such as format, type, range, or consistency. Cleaning means removing or correcting any invalid, missing, or erroneous data. Validation and cleaning are important steps to ensure the quality and integrity of the data, and to prevent any further errors or problems in the data processing.

The techniques for validating and cleaning data depend on the type and structure of the data, and the requirements and specifications of the data processing. However, some general steps that you can follow are:

- Define the rules or criteria for valid data, such as the expected format, type, range, or consistency of the data elements.
- Use the `try` and `except` statements to catch any errors or exceptions that may occur during the data processing, and handle them appropriately.
- Use the `if` and `else` statements to check if the data meets the rules or criteria, and handle any invalid data accordingly.
- Use the built-in functions or modules, such as `int()`, `float()`, `str()`, `re`, or `csv`, to convert, parse, or manipulate the data elements as needed.
- Use the `strip()`, `replace()`, `lower()`, `upper()`, or `title()` methods to remove or modify any unwanted characters or whitespace from the data elements as needed.
- Use the `isinstance()`, `isnumeric()`, `isalpha()`, `isalnum()`, or `isdecimal()` methods to check the type or format of the data elements as needed.
- Use the `len()`, `min()`, `max()`, `sum()`, `mean()`, `median()`, `mode()`, or `std()` functions or modules, such as `statistics`, to calculate or verify the length, range, or statistics of the data elements as needed.
- Use the `print()`, `assert()`, or `logging` functions or modules to display, test, or log the data elements as needed.

For example, suppose you want to read a file named `data.txt` that contains some numerical data separated by commas, and you want to validate and clean the data before performing some calculations. The rules or criteria for valid data are:

- The data should be numeric, not alphanumeric or symbolic.
- The data should be positive, not negative or zero.
- The data should be within the range of 1 to 100, not outside or beyond.

You can use the following code to read, validate, and clean the data:

```
file = open('data.txt', 'r')
lines = file.readlines()
file.close()
```

```
data = []
for line in lines:
    elements = line.split(',')
    for element in elements:
        try:
            element = float(element.strip())
            if element > 0 and element <= 100:
                data.append(element)
            else:
                print(f'Invalid data: {element} is out of
range.')
        except ValueError:
            print(f'Invalid data: {element} is not numeric.')
print(data)
```

# Validating and Cleaning Data

Sometimes, you may want to validate and clean the data while reading from the file, instead of storing the data in a list and processing it later. This can save memory and time, especially if the file is large or the data is complex. To do this, you can use a generator function or expression to yield the data elements one by one, after validating and cleaning them. A generator function or expression is a special type of function or expression that can produce a sequence of values, without storing them in memory. You can use the `yield` keyword to return a value from a generator function or expression, and use the `next()` function or a `for` loop to get the next value from the generator.

For example, suppose you want to read a file named `data.txt` that contains some numerical data separated by commas, and you want to validate and clean the data while reading from the file. You can use the following generator function to yield the data elements one by one:

```
def read_data(filename):
    file = open(filename, 'r')
    lines = file.readlines()
    file.close()
    for line in lines:
        elements = line.split(',')
        for element in elements:
            try:
                element = float(element.strip())
                if element > 0 and element <= 100:
                    yield element
```

```
                else:
                    print(f'Invalid data: {element} is out of
range.')
            except ValueError:
                print(f'Invalid data: {element} is not
numeric.')
```

You can then use the generator function to get the data elements as needed. For example, to print the data elements, you can write:

```
data = read_data('data.txt')
for element in data:
    print(element)
```

Alternatively, you can use a generator expression to achieve the same result. A generator expression is like a list comprehension, but uses parentheses instead of brackets, and does not create a list in memory. For example, you can write:

```
data = (float(element.strip()) for line in open('data.txt',
'r') for element in line.split(',') if
element.strip().isnumeric() and 0 < float(element.strip()) <=
100)
for element in data:
    print(element)
```

# Formatting and Transforming Data

Sometimes, you may want to format and transform the data before writing to the file, instead of writing the data as it is. This can make the data more compatible with different file formats, such as CSV, JSON, or XML, or more readable and understandable for the users. To do this, you can use various techniques and methods to convert, parse, or manipulate the data elements as needed, before writing them to the file.

For example, suppose you want to write a list of dictionaries to a file named `output.txt`, and you want to format and transform the data to match the JSON format. JSON (JavaScript Object Notation) is a popular file format that can store structured data as a collection of key-value pairs, enclosed by curly braces (`{}`), and separated by commas (`,`). You can use the following code to format and transform the data before writing to the file:

```
import json
data = [{'name': 'Alice', 'age': 25, 'gender': 'F'}, {'name':
```

```
'Bob', 'age': 30, 'gender': 'M'}, {'name': 'Charlie', 'age':
35, 'gender': 'M'}]
file = open('output.txt', 'w')
file.write(json.dumps(data))
file.close()
```

Note that the `json` module provides various functions and methods to work with JSON data in Python. The `json.dumps()` function converts a Python object, such as a list or a dictionary, to a JSON-formatted string. The `json.loads()` function does the opposite, converting a JSON-formatted string to a Python object. You can use these functions to read and write JSON data from or to a file.

# Reading and Writing JSON Files

JSON (JavaScript Object Notation) is a popular format for storing and exchanging structured data. JSON files are composed of key-value pairs, which can be nested, and arrays, which can contain any type of values. JSON files can be easily parsed and generated by various programming languages, including Python.

## JSON vs Pandas

There are several libraries available in Python for working with JSON files, but two of the most common and widely used ones are json and pandas. Both libraries provide functions for reading and writing JSON data from and to files, but they have some differences in features, performance, and compatibility.

json is a built-in library in Python, which means that you do not need to install any external dependencies to use it. It implements the JSON standard, and supports basic operations such as loading, dumping, encoding, and decoding JSON data. It also supports customizing the serialization and deserialization process by using hooks, such as `object_hook` and `default`.

pandas is an external library that you need to install separately, using pip or other tools. It is a powerful and versatile library for data analysis and manipulation, which provides high-level data structures and operations, such as `DataFrame` and `Series`. It supports reading and writing JSON data from and to files, as well as other formats, such as CSV, Excel, HTML, etc. It also supports various options and parameters for controlling the input and output format, such as `orient`, `lines`, `compression`, etc.

The main advantages of using pandas over json are:

- pandas is faster and more memory-efficient than json, especially for large or complex JSON files.
- pandas provides more features and flexibility than json, such as handling missing values, converting data types, filtering and sorting data, applying functions, etc.

- pandas has a more consistent and user-friendly API than json, and provides some convenience methods and attributes that make working with JSON data easier.
- The main disadvantages of using pandas over json are:
- pandas is not a built-in library in Python, and requires installation of external dependencies, which may not be available or compatible on some platforms or environments.
- pandas may raise different exceptions or errors than json, which may require some changes in the error handling code.
- pandas may not be compatible with some third-party libraries or tools that expect or use json objects.

In summary, pandas is a more powerful and feature-rich library than json, but it also has some drawbacks in terms of installation, compatibility, and consistency. Depending on your needs and preferences, you may choose to use either library for working with JSON files in Python. In this chapter, we will use pandas as our default library, but we will also show how to use json for some basic operations.

# Serialization in Python

Serialization is converting a Python object, such as a dictionary, a list, or a custom class, into a format that can be stored or transmitted, such as a string, a byte stream, or a file. Deserialization is the reverse process of converting a serialized format back into a Python object.

Serialization is useful for reading and writing complex data structures to files, such as JSON files. It is also useful for sending and receiving data over a network, such as a web service or an API.

There are different ways of serializing and deserializing Python objects, depending on the format and the library. For example, to serialize and deserialize a Python object to and from a JSON file, you can use the `json` or `pandas` library, as we will see in the next sections. To serialize and deserialize a Python object to and from a binary file, you can use the `pickle` library, which is a built-in library in Python that implements a binary protocol for serialization and deserialization.

The `pickle` library provides functions such as `dump`, `load`, `dumps`, and `loads` for serializing and deserializing Python objects to and from files or strings. The `pickle` library can handle most Python objects, such as numbers, strings, lists, dictionaries, tuples, sets, functions, classes, etc. However, it cannot handle some objects, such as generators, closures, lambda functions, etc. It also has some limitations and risks, such as compatibility issues, security issues, and performance issues.

The main advantages of using `pickle` over other formats and libraries are:

- `pickle` can serialize and deserialize most Python objects, including custom classes and functions, without losing any information or functionality.
- `pickle` can preserve the internal state and structure of Python objects, such as references, inheritance, attributes, methods, etc.
- `pickle` can compress the data and reduce the file size, by using different protocols and compression levels.

The main disadvantages of using `pickle` over other formats and libraries are:

- `pickle` is not a human-readable or cross-language format, and can only be used by Python programs.
- `pickle` is not a stable or standardized format, and can change across different versions of Python or `pickle`, which may cause compatibility issues or errors.
- `pickle` is not a secure or reliable format, and can execute arbitrary code or cause data corruption, if the source or the content of the file is not trusted or verified.

# Reading and Parsing JSON Data

To read and parse JSON data from a file in Python, you can use the `read_json` function from pandas, or the `load` or `loads` function from json. The `read_json` function takes a file name or a file object as an argument, and returns a `DataFrame` or a `Series` object, depending on the input format. The `load` function takes a file object as an argument, and returns a Python object, such as a dictionary or a list, depending on the input format. The `loads` function takes a string as an argument, and returns a

Python object, depending on the input format.

For example, to read and parse the JSON file `movies.json`, which contains information about some movies, you can write:

```
import pandas as pd
import json
df = pd.read_json('movies.json') # returns a DataFrame object
# or
with open('movies.json', 'r') as f:
    data = json.load(f) # returns a dictionary object
# or
s = '{"movie": "The Matrix", "director": "Wachowski, Lana and Lilly", "genre": "Sci-Fi", "price": 9.99, "release_date": "1999-03-31", "description": "A computer hacker learns from mysterious rebels about the true nature of his reality and his role in the war against its controllers."}'
data = json.loads(s) # returns a dictionary object
```

The JSON file `movies.json` could look something like this:

```
[
  {
    "movie": "The Matrix",
    "director": "Wachowski, Lana and Lilly",
    "genre": "Sci-Fi",
    "price": 9.99,
    "release_date": "1999-03-31",
    "description": "A computer hacker learns from mysterious rebels about the true nature of his reality and his role in the war against its controllers."
  },
  {
    "movie": "The Lord of the Rings: The Fellowship of the Ring",
    "director": "Jackson, Peter",
    "genre": "Fantasy",
    "price": 12.99,
    "release_date": "2001-12-19",
    "description": "A meek Hobbit from the Shire and eight companions set out on a journey to destroy the powerful One Ring and save Middle-earth from the Dark Lord Sauron."
  },
  {
    "movie": "The Godfather",
    "director": "Coppola, Francis Ford",
    "genre": "Crime",
```

```
    "price": 14.99,
    "release_date": "1972-03-24",
    "description": "The aging patriarch of an organized crime dynasty transfers control of his clandestine empire to his reluctant son."
  }
]
```

To access the data from the `DataFrame` or the `Series` object, you can use the methods and attributes of pandas, such as `head`, `tail`, `loc`, `iloc`, `columns`, `index`, etc. For example, to get the first five rows of the `DataFrame` object, you can write:

```
df.head()
```

| movie | director | genre | price | release_date | description |
|---|---|---|---|---|---|
| The Matrix | Wachowski, Lana and Lilly | Sci-Fi | 9.99 | 1999-03-31 | A computer hacker learns from mysterious rebels about the true nature of his reality and his role in the war against its controllers. |
| The Lord of the Rings: The Fellowship of the Ring | Jackson, Peter | Fantasy | 12.99 | 2001-12-19 | A meek Hobbit from the Shire and eight companions set out on a journey to destroy the powerful One Ring and save Middle-earth from the Dark Lord Sauron. |
| The Godfather | Coppola, Francis Ford | Crime | 14.99 | 1972-03- | The aging patriarch of an organized |

| | | | | | |
|---|---|---|---|---|---|
| | | | | 24 | crime dynasty transfers control of his clandestine empire to his reluctant son. |
| The Shawshank Redemption | Darabont, Frank | Drama | 9.99 | 1994-09-23 | Two imprisoned men bond over a number of years, finding solace and eventual redemption through acts of common decency. |
| The Dark Knight | Nolan, Christopher | Action | 14.99 | 2008-07-18 | When the menace known as the Joker wreaks havoc and chaos on the people of Gotham, Batman must accept one of the greatest psychological and physical tests of his ability to fight injustice. |

To access the data from the dictionary or the list object, you can use the standard Python syntax and operations, such as indexing, slicing, looping, etc. For example, to get the title of the first movie from the dictionary object, you can write:

```
data[0]['movie']
```

To parse a JSON string, you can use the `read_json` function from pandas with the `typ` parameter set to `'series'`, or the `loads` function from json. For example, to parse the JSON string `s`, which contains information about a movie, you can write:

```
import pandas as pd
import json
series = pd.read_json(s, typ='series') # returns a Series
object
# or
data = json.loads(s) # returns a dictionary object
```

# Writing JSON Data to Files

To write JSON data to a file in Python, you can use the `to_json` method from pandas, or the `dump` or `dumps` function from json. The `to_json` method takes a file name or a file object as an argument, and optionally some parameters such as `orient`, `lines`, `compression`, etc. to control the output format. The `dump` function takes a Python object, such as a dictionary or a list, and a file object as arguments, and optionally some parameters such as `indent`, `sort_keys`, `ensure_ascii`, etc. to control the output format. The `dumps` function takes a Python object as an argument, and returns a string, with the same optional parameters as the `dump` function.

For example, to write the `DataFrame` object `df` to a JSON file `movies.json`, you can write:

```
import pandas as pd
import json
df.to_json('movies.json') # writes a JSON file with the
default format
# or
with open('movies.json', 'w') as f:
    json.dump(df.to_dict(orient='records'), f) # writes a
JSON file with a list of dictionaries format
# or
s = json.dumps(df.to_dict(orient='records'), indent=4,
sort_keys=True) # returns a JSON string with a list of
dictionaries format, indented and sorted
```

To write a dictionary object `data` to a JSON file `movie.json`, you can write:

```
import pandas as pd
import json
with open('movie.json', 'w') as f:
```

```
    json.dump(data, f) # writes a JSON file with the default
format
# or
s = json.dumps(data, indent=4, sort_keys=True) # returns a
JSON string with the default format, indented and sorted
```

To write a JSON string `s` to a JSON file `movie.json`, you can write:

```
import pandas as pd
import json
with open('movie.json', 'w') as f:
    f.write(s) # writes a JSON file with the same format as
the string
# or
data = json.loads(s) # converts the JSON string to a Python
object
with open('movie.json', 'w') as f:
    json.dump(data, f) # writes a JSON file with the default
format
```

## Handling Nested, Array, and Null Values

JSON files can contain nested, array, and null values, which can pose some challenges for reading and writing JSON data in Python. In this section, we will explore some techniques for handling these values in Python.

### Nested Values

Nested values are values that contain other values, such as dictionaries or lists. For example, consider the following JSON file, which contains information about some students and their courses:

```
[
  {
    "name": "Alice",
    "age": 20,
    "courses": [
      {
        "name": "Math",
        "grade": 90
      },
      {
        "name": "English",
        "grade": 85
      }
    ]
```

```
  },
  {
    "name": "Bob",
    "age": 21,
    "courses": [
      {
        "name": "Physics",
        "grade": 95
      },
      {
        "name": "History",
        "grade": 80
      }
    ]
  }
]
```

The JSON file contains a list of dictionaries, each representing a student. Each student has a name, an age, and a list of courses. Each course is a dictionary, containing a name and a grade.

To read and parse this JSON file in Python, you can use the `read_json` function from pandas, or the `load` or `loads` function from json, as we have seen in the previous section. For example, to read and parse the JSON file `students.json`, you can write:

```
import pandas as pd
import json
df = pd.read_json('students.json') # returns a DataFrame
object
# or
with open('students.json', 'r') as f:
    data = json.load(f) # returns a list of dictionaries
object
# or
s = '[{"name": "Alice", "age": 20, "courses": [{"name":
"Math", "grade": 90}, {"name": "English", "grade": 85}]},
{"name": "Bob", "age": 21, "courses": [{"name": "Physics",
"grade": 95}, {"name": "History", "grade": 80}]}]'
data = json.loads(s) # returns a list of dictionaries object
```

To access the nested values from the `DataFrame` object, you can use the methods and attributes of pandas, such as `loc`, `iloc`, `columns`, `index`, etc. For example, to get the name and grade of the first course of the first student, you can write:

```
df.loc[0, 'courses'][0]['name'] # returns 'Math'
df.loc[0, 'courses'][0]['grade'] # returns 90
```

To access the nested values from the list of dictionaries object, you can use the standard Python syntax and operations, such as indexing, slicing, looping, etc. For example, to get the name and grade of the first course of the first student, you can write:

```
data[0]['courses'][0]['name'] # returns 'Math'
data[0]['courses'][0]['grade'] # returns 90
```

To write the nested values to a JSON file in Python, you can use the `to_json` method from pandas, or the `dump` or `dumps` function from json, as we have seen in the previous section. For example, to write the `DataFrame` object `df` to a JSON file `students.json`, you can write:

```
import pandas as pd
import json
df.to_json('students.json') # writes a JSON file with the
default format
# or
with open('students.json', 'w') as f:
    json.dump(df.to_dict(orient='records'), f) # writes a
JSON file with a list of dictionaries format
# or
s = json.dumps(df.to_dict(orient='records'), indent=4,
sort_keys=True) # returns a JSON string with a list of
dictionaries format, indented and sorted
```

To write a list of dictionaries object `data` to a JSON file `students.json`, you can write:

```
import pandas as pd
import json
with open('students.json', 'w') as f:
    json.dump(data, f) # writes a JSON file with the default
format
# or
s = json.dumps(data, indent=4, sort_keys=True) # returns a
JSON string with the default format, indented and sorted
```

To write a JSON string `s` to a JSON file `students.json`, you can write:

```
import pandas as pd
import json
```

```
with open('students.json', 'w') as f:
    f.write(s) # writes a JSON file with the same format as
the string
# or
data = json.loads(s) # converts the JSON string to a Python
object
with open('students.json', 'w') as f:
    json.dump(data, f) # writes a JSON file with the default
format
```

## Array Values

Array values are values that contain a sequence of values, such as lists or tuples. For example, consider the following JSON file, which contains information about some products and their prices:

```
[
  {
    "product": "Laptop",
    "price": 999.99,
    "features": ["Intel Core i7", "16 GB RAM", "512 GB SSD",
"15.6 inch FHD"]
  },
  {
    "product": "Smartphone",
    "price": 699.99,
    "features": ["Snapdragon 888", "8 GB RAM", "256 GB ROM",
"6.7 inch AMOLED"]
  },
  {
    "product": "Headphones",
    "price": 199.99,
    "features": ["Bluetooth 5.0", "Noise Cancelling",
"Wireless Charging", "24 Hours Battery"]
  }
]
```

The JSON file contains a list of dictionaries, each representing a product. Each product has a name, a price, and a list of features.

To read and parse this JSON file in Python, you can use the `read_json` function from pandas, or the `load` or `loads` function from json, as we have seen in the previous section. For example, to read and parse the JSON file `products.json`, you can write:

```
import pandas as pd
```

```
import json
df = pd.read_json('products.json') # returns a DataFrame
object
# or
with open('products.json', 'r') as f:
    data = json.load(f) # returns a list of dictionaries
object
# or
s = '[{"product": "Laptop", "price": 999.99, "features":
["Intel Core i7", "16 GB RAM", "512 GB SSD", "15.6 inch
FHD"]}, {"product": "Smartphone", "price": 699.99,
"features": ["Snapdragon 888", "8 GB RAM", "256 GB ROM", "6.7
inch AMOLED"]}, {"product": "Headphones", "price": 199.99,
"features": ["Bluetooth 5.0", "Noise Cancelling","Wireless
Charging", "24 Hours Battery"]}]' data = json.loads(s) #
returns a list of dictionaries object
```

To access the array values from the `DataFrame` object, you can use the methods and attributes of pandas, such as `loc`, `iloc`, `columns`, `index`, etc. For example, to get the first feature of the first product, you can write:

```
df.loc[0, 'features'][0] # returns 'Intel Core i7'
```

To access the array values from the list of dictionaries object, you can use the standard Python syntax and operations, such as indexing, slicing, looping, etc. For example, to get the first feature of the first product, you can write:

```
data[0]['features'][0] # returns 'Intel Core i7'
```

To write the array values to a JSON file in Python, you can use the `to_json` method from pandas, or the `dump` or `dumps` function from json, as we have seen in the previous section. For example, to write the `DataFrame` object `df` to a JSON file `products.json`, you can write:

```
import pandas as pd
import json
df.to_json('products.json') # writes a JSON file with the
default format
# or
with open('products.json', 'w') as f:
    json.dump(df.to_dict(orient='records'), f) # writes a
JSON file with a list of dictionaries format
# or
s = json.dumps(df.to_dict(orient='records'), indent=4,
```

```
sort_keys=True) # returns a JSON string with a list of
dictionaries format, indented and sorted
```

To write a list of dictionaries object `data` to a JSON file `products.json`, you can write:

```
import pandas as pd
import json
with open('products.json', 'w') as f:
    json.dump(data, f) # writes a JSON file with the default
format
# or
s = json.dumps(data, indent=4, sort_keys=True) # returns a
JSON string with the default format, indented and sorted
```

To write a JSON string `s` to a JSON file `products.json`, you can write:

```
import pandas as pd
import json
with open('products.json', 'w') as f:
    f.write(s) # writes a JSON file with the same format as
the string
# or
data = json.loads(s) # converts the JSON string to a Python
object
with open('products.json', 'w') as f:
    json.dump(data, f) # writes a JSON file with the default
format
```

## Null Values

Null values are values that represent the absence of any value, such as `None` in Python or `null` in JSON. For example, consider the following JSON file, which contains information about some employees and their salaries:

```
[
  {
    "name": "Alice",
    "age": 25,
    "salary": 5000
  },
  {
    "name": "Bob",
    "age": 30,
    "salary": null
  },
```

```
  {
    "name": "Charlie",
    "age": 35,
    "salary": 7000
  }
]
```

The JSON file contains a list of dictionaries, each representing an employee. Each employee has a name, an age, and a salary. The salary of Bob is `null`, which means that it is unknown or missing.

To read and parse this JSON file in Python, you can use the `read_json` function from pandas, or the `load` or `loads` function from json, as we have seen in the previous section. For example, to read and parse the JSON file `employees.json`, you can write:

```
import pandas as pd
import json
df = pd.read_json('employees.json') # returns a DataFrame
object
# or
with open('employees.json', 'r') as f:
    data = json.load(f) # returns a list of dictionaries
object
# or
s = '[{"name": "Alice", "age": 25, "salary": 5000}, {"name":
"Bob", "age": 30, "salary": null}, {"name": "Charlie", "age":
35, "salary": 7000}]'
data = json.loads(s) # returns a list of dictionaries object
```

To handle the null values from the `DataFrame` object, you can use the methods and attributes of pandas, such as `isnull`, `notnull`, `dropna`, `fillna`, etc. For example, to check whether the salary of each employee is null, you can write:

```
df['salary'].isnull() # returns a Series object with True or
False values
```

To handle the null values from the list of dictionaries object, you can use the standard Python syntax and operations, such as `None`, `is`, `is not`, etc. For example, to check whether the salary of each employee is null, you can write:

```
for employee in data:
```

```
    if employee['salary'] is None: # or if employee['salary']
is not None:
        # do something
```

To write the null values to a JSON file in Python, you can use the `to_json` method from pandas, or the `dump` or `dumps` function from json, as we have seen in the previous section. For example, to write the `DataFrame` object `df` to a JSON file `employees.json`, you can write:

```
import pandas as pd
import json
df.to_json('employees.json') # writes a JSON file with the
default format
# or
with open('employees.json', 'w') as f:
    json.dump(df.to_dict(orient='records'), f) # writes a
JSON file with a list of dictionaries format
# or
s = json.dumps(df.to_dict(orient='records'), indent=4,
sort_keys=True) # returns a JSON string with a list of
dictionaries format, indented and sorted
```

To write a list of dictionaries object `data` to a JSON file `employees.json`, you can write:

```
import pandas as pd
import json
with open('employees.json', 'w') as f:
    json.dump(data, f) # writes a JSON file with the default
format
# or
s = json.dumps(data, indent=4, sort_keys=True) # returns a
JSON string with the default format, indented and sorted
```

To write a JSON string `s` to a JSON file `employees.json`, you can write:

```
import pandas as pd
import json
with open('employees.json', 'w') as f:
    f.write(s) # writes a JSON file with the same format as
the string
# or
data = json.loads(s) # converts the JSON string to a Python
object
with open('employees.json', 'w') as f:
```

```
    json.dump(data, f) # writes a JSON file with the default
format
```

# Pretty-Printing, Indenting, and Compressing JSON Data

JSON data can be formatted in different ways, such as pretty-printing, indenting, and compressing, to improve the readability, clarity, and size of the data. In this section, we will explore some techniques for formatting JSON data in Python.

## Pretty-Printing

Pretty-printing is the process of formatting JSON data in a way that makes it easier to read and understand, by adding spaces, newlines, and indentation. For example, consider the following JSON data, which contains information about some products and their prices:

```
[{"product":"Laptop","price":999.99,"features":["Intel Core
i7","16 GB RAM","512 GB SSD","15.6 inch FHD"]},
{"product":"Smartphone","price":699.99,"features":
["Snapdragon 888","8 GB RAM","256 GB ROM","6.7 inch
AMOLED"]},{"product":"Headphones","price":199.99,"features":
["Bluetooth 5.0","Noise Cancelling","Wireless Charging","24
Hours Battery"]}]
```

The JSON data is not easy to read or understand, as it is compressed into a single line, without any spaces or indentation. A pretty-printed version of the JSON data would look something like this:

```
[
  {
    "product": "Laptop",
    "price": 999.99,
    "features": [
      "Intel Core i7",
      "16 GB RAM",
      "512 GB SSD",
      "15.6 inch FHD"
    ]
  },
  {
    "product": "Smartphone",
    "price": 699.99,
```

```
    "features": [
      "Snapdragon 888",
      "8 GB RAM",
      "256 GB ROM",
      "6.7 inch AMOLED"
    ]
  },
  {
    "product": "Headphones",
    "price": 199.99,
    "features": [
      "Bluetooth 5.0",
      "Noise Cancelling",
      "Wireless Charging",
      "24 Hours Battery"
    ]
  }
]
```

The pretty-printed version of the JSON data is easier to read and understand, as it is formatted into multiple lines, with spaces and indentation.

To pretty-print JSON data in Python, you can use the `indent` parameter from the `to_json` method from pandas, or the `dump` or `dumps` function from json. The `indent` parameter takes an integer value that specifies the number of spaces to use for indentation. For example:

```
import json

# Assume 'data' is a dictionary containing our JSON data
data = {
    "name": "John Doe",
    "age": 30,
    "is_employee": True,
    "skills": ["Python", "Data Analysis", "Machine
Learning"],
    "salary": None
}

# Convert the Python dictionary to a pretty-printed JSON
string
pretty_printed_json = json.dumps(data, indent=4)

# Print the pretty-printed JSON string
print(pretty_printed_json)
```

When you run this code, it will output the JSON data with an indentation of 4 spaces, which makes it much easier to read:

```
{
    "name": "John Doe",
    "age": 30,
    "is_employee": true,
    "skills": [
        "Python",
        "Data Analysis",
        "Machine Learning"
    ],
    "salary": null
}
```

As you can see, each level of the JSON structure is indented with 4 spaces, which visually separates the keys and values, making the data hierarchy clear. This is especially helpful when dealing with nested JSON objects.

## Compressing

Compressing JSON data is about reducing its size, which can be useful for storage or transmission purposes. This typically involves removing unnecessary whitespace. Here's how you can compress JSON data:

```
import json

# Assuming 'data' is your JSON object
compressed_json = json.dumps(data, separators=(',', ':'))
print(compressed_json)
```

The `separators` parameter is a tuple that tells the `json.dumps` function to use a comma and a colon as separators without any spaces, thus minimizing the size of the JSON string.

## Pretty-Printing with pandas

If you're using the `pandas` library, you can also pretty-print JSON data when converting a `DataFrame` to a JSON string:

```
import pandas as pd

# Assuming 'df' is your DataFrame
pretty_json = df.to_json(orient='records', lines=True,
indent=4)
print(pretty_json)
```

This will output a JSON string that is formatted with an indentation of 4 spaces per level, with each record on a new line.

In summary, pretty-printing, indenting, and compressing are valuable techniques for working with JSON data in Python. They can improve the readability of the data, make it easier to debug, and optimize it for storage and transmission. By using the `json` and `pandas` libraries, you can easily apply these techniques to your JSON data handling processes.

# Reading and Writing CSV Files

CSV files are a staple in data storage and manipulation. Python provides two main libraries for handling CSV files: the built-in `csv` module and the third-party `pandas` library. Below, we'll explore how to use these libraries with code examples and expected outputs.

## Reading Data from CSV Files

### Using the csv Module

The `csv` module allows you to read CSV files line by line.

```
import csv

# Sample CSV content:
# Name,Age
# Alice,24
# Bob,27

# Reading the CSV file
with open('example.csv', mode='r') as file:
    csv_reader = csv.reader(file)
    for row in csv_reader:
        print(row)

# Output:
# ['Name', 'Age']
# ['Alice', '24']
# ['Bob', '27']
```

### Using pandas

`pandas` simplifies the process by reading the entire file into a DataFrame, which is a 2-dimensional labeled data structure.

```
import pandas as pd

# Reading the CSV file into a DataFrame
df = pd.read_csv('example.csv')

# Displaying the DataFrame
print(df)
```

```
# Output:
#      Name  Age
# 0   Alice   24
# 1     Bob   27
```

# Writing Data to CSV Files

## Using the csv Module

You can write to CSV files using the `csv` module by specifying each row as a list.

```
import csv

# Data to be written
data = [['Name', 'Age'], ['Alice', 24], ['Bob', 27]]

# Writing to the CSV file
with open('output.csv', mode='w', newline='') as file:
    csv_writer = csv.writer(file)
    csv_writer.writerows(data)

# The 'output.csv' file now contains:
# Name,Age
# Alice,24
# Bob,27
```

## Using pandas

`pandas` provides a method to export a DataFrame to a CSV file.

```
import pandas as pd

# Creating a DataFrame
df = pd.DataFrame(data[1:], columns=data[0])

# Writing the DataFrame to a CSV file
df.to_csv('output.csv', index=False)

# The 'output.csv' file now contains:
# Name,Age
# Alice,24
# Bob,27
```

# XML Files

XML (Extensible Markup Language) is a widely used format for storing and exchanging structured data. XML files are composed of tags, which define the structure and meaning of the data, and text, which contains the actual data. XML files can be validated against schemas, which specify the rules and constraints for the data, and transformed using XSLT (Extensible Stylesheet Language Transformations), which define how to convert the data from one format to another.

## xml.etree.ElementTree vs lxml

There are several libraries available in Python for working with XML files, but two of the most popular and widely used ones are xml.etree.ElementTree and lxml. Both libraries provide a similar interface for accessing and manipulating XML data, but they have some differences in features, performance, and compatibility.

xml.etree.ElementTree is a built-in library in Python, so you do not need to install any external dependencies to use it. It implements a subset of the XML standard, and supports basic operations, such as parsing, searching, modifying, and creating XML data. It also supports XML namespaces, which are prefixes that identify the source or context of the tags and attributes.

lxml is an external library that you need to install separately, using pip or other tools. It is based on libxml2 and libxslt, which are C libraries that implement the full XML standard. It supports all the features of xml.etree.ElementTree, and also provides some additional features, such as XPath, XSLT, validation, and parsing HTML. It also supports XML namespaces, and has some extensions that make working with namespaces easier.

The main advantages of using lxml over xml.etree.ElementTree are:

- lxml is faster and more memory-efficient than xml.etree.ElementTree, especially for large or complex XML files.
- lxml supports more XML features and standards than xml.etree.ElementTree, such as XPath, XSLT, validation, and parsing

HTML.

- lxml has a more consistent and user-friendly API than xml.etree.ElementTree, and provides some convenience methods and classes that make working with XML data easier.

The main disadvantages of using lxml over xml.etree.ElementTree are:

- lxml is not a built-in library in Python, and requires installation of external dependencies, which may not be available or compatible on some platforms or environments.
- lxml may raise different exceptions or errors than xml.etree.ElementTree, which may require some changes in the error handling code.
- lxml may not be compatible with some third-party libraries or tools that expect or use xml.etree.ElementTree objects.

lxml is a more powerful and feature-rich library than xml.etree.ElementTree, but it also has some drawbacks in terms of installation, compatibility, and consistency. Depending on your needs and preferences, you may choose to use either library for working with XML files in Python.

## Parsing, Modifying, and Creating XML Data

To read and write XML data from and to files, you can use the `parse` and `write` functions from lxml or xml.etree.ElementTree. The `parse` function takes a file name or a file object as an argument, and returns an `ElementTree` object, which represents the whole XML tree. The `write` function takes an `ElementTree` object, a file name or a file object, and optionally some parameters such as encoding, xml_declaration, pretty_print, etc. as arguments, and writes the XML data to the file.

For example, to parse the XML file `books.xml` and write it to a new file `books_copy.xml`, you can write:

```
from lxml import etree
tree = etree.parse('books.xml')
tree.write('books_copy.xml', encoding='UTF-8',
xml_declaration=True, pretty_print=True)
```

To create a new XML data from scratch, you can use the `Element` and `SubElement` constructors, and the `ElementTree` constructor. For example, to create a new XML data with information about some movies, you can write:

```
from lxml import etree
catalog = etree.Element('catalog')
movie = etree.SubElement(catalog, 'movie', id='mv101')
title = etree.SubElement(movie, 'title')
title.text = 'The Matrix'
director = etree.SubElement(movie, 'director')
director.text = 'Wachowski, Lana and Lilly'
genre = etree.SubElement(movie, 'genre')
genre.text = 'Sci-Fi'
price = etree.SubElement(movie, 'price')
price.text = '9.99'
release_date = etree.SubElement(movie, 'release_date')
release_date.text = '1999-03-31'
description = etree.SubElement(movie, 'description')
description.text = 'A computer hacker learns from mysterious
rebels about the true nature of his reality and his role in
the war against its controllers.'
tree = etree.ElementTree(catalog)
tree.write('movies.xml', encoding='UTF-8',
xml_declaration=True, pretty_print=True)
```

To modify the XML data, you can use the methods and attributes of the `Element` and `ElementTree` objects, as we have seen in the previous section. For example, to change the title of the first book to `'Python Developer's Guide'`, you can write:

```
from lxml import etree
tree = etree.parse('books.xml')
root = tree.getroot()
first_book = root.find('book')
first_title =
first_book.find('{http://example.com/book}title')
first_title.text = 'Python Developer's Guide'
tree.write('books_modified.xml', encoding='UTF-8',
xml_declaration=True, pretty_print=True)
```

# XML Tree, Elements, Attributes, and Namespaces

The core concept of both lxml and xml.etree.ElementTree is the XML tree, which is a hierarchical representation of the XML data. The XML tree consists of nodes, which are objects that store information about the data. The most common type of node is the element, which corresponds to a tag in the XML file. An element can have a tag name, a text value, a set of attributes, and a list of child elements. An attribute is a key-value pair that provides additional information about an element. A namespace is a prefix that identifies the source or context of the tag name or attribute name.

For example, consider the following XML file, which contains information about some books:

```
<?xml version="1.0" encoding="UTF-8"?>
<catalog xmlns:bk="http://example.com/book">
  <book id="bk101">
    <bk:title>XML Developer's Guide</bk:title>
    <bk:author>Gambardella, Matthew</bk:author>
    <bk:genre>Computer</bk:genre>
    <bk:price>44.95</bk:price>
    <bk:publish_date>2000-10-01</bk:publish_date>
    <bk:description>An in-depth look at creating applications
with XML.</bk:description>
  </book>
  <book id="bk102">
    <bk:title>Midnight Rain</bk:title>
    <bk:author>Ralls, Kim</bk:author>
    <bk:genre>Fantasy</bk:genre>
    <bk:price>5.95</bk:price>
    <bk:publish_date>2000-12-16</bk:publish_date>
    <bk:description>A former architect battles corporate
zombies, an evil sorceress, and her own childhood to become
queen of the world.</bk:description>
  </book>
</catalog>
```

The XML tree for this file would look something like this:

```
catalog
├── book
│   ├── bk:title
│   ├── bk:author
│   ├── bk:genre
│   ├── bk:price
│   ├── bk:publish_date
│   └── bk:description
└── book
    ├── bk:title
    ├── bk:author
    │
```

```
├── bk:genre
├── bk:price
├── bk:publish_date
└── bk:description
```

The root element of the XML tree is `catalog`, which has two child elements, `book`. Each `book` element has an attribute `id`, and six child elements, `bk:title`, `bk:author`, `bk:genre`, `bk:price`, `bk:publish_date`, and `bk:description`. The prefix `bk` is a namespace that indicates that the tag names and attribute names are from the `http://example.com/book` URI.

In lxml and xml.etree.ElementTree, an element is represented by an `Element` object, which has the following attributes and methods:

- `tag`: the tag name of the element, as a string. If the element has a namespace, the tag name will include the namespace URI in curly braces, such as `'{http://example.com/book}title'`.
- `text`: the text value of the element, as a string. If the element has no text, the value will be `None`.
- `tail`: the text value that follows the element, as a string. If the element has no tail, the value will be `None`.
- `attrib`: a dictionary that contains the attributes of the element, as key-value pairs. If the attribute has a namespace, the key will include the namespace URI in curly braces, such as `'{http://example.com/book}id'`.
- `get(key, default=None)`: a method that returns the value of the attribute with the given key, or the default value if the attribute does not exist.
- `set(key, value)`: a method that sets the value of the attribute with the given key, or creates a new attribute if the key does not exist.
- `find(match)`: a method that returns the first child element that matches the given tag name or XPath expression, or `None` if no match is found.
- `findall(match)`: a method that returns a list of all child elements that match the given tag name or XPath expression, or an empty list if no

match is found.

- `iterfind(match)`: a method that returns an iterator over all child elements that match the given tag name or XPath expression, or an empty iterator if no match is found.
- `iter(tag=None)`: a method that returns an iterator over all descendant elements with the given tag name, or all descendant elements if no tag name is given.
- `append(element)`: a method that adds a new child element to the end of the element's children.
- `insert(index, element)`: a method that inserts a new child element at the given index in the element's children.
- `remove(element)`: a method that removes a child element from the element's children.
- `clear()`: a method that removes all the attributes and child elements from the element.

To create an `Element` object, you can use the `Element` constructor, which takes the tag name and optionally the attributes as arguments. For example, to create an element with the tag name `'{http://example.com/book}title'` and the text value `'XML Developer's Guide'`, you can write:

```
from lxml import etree
title = etree.Element('{http://example.com/book}title')
title.text = 'XML Developer's Guide'
help(title) #to see all available methods and their usage
```

Alternatively, you can use the `SubElement` constructor, which takes the parent element and the tag name as arguments, and optionally the attributes and the text value. For example, to create a child element with the tag name `'{http://example.com/book}author'` and the text value `'Ralls, Kim'`, you can write:

```
from lxml import etree
author = etree.SubElement(book,
'{http://example.com/book}author')
author.text = 'Ralls, Kim'
```

To access the attributes of an element, you can use the `attrib` dictionary or the `get` method. For example, to get the value of the `id` attribute of the `book` element, you can write:

```
book_id = book.attrib['{http://example.com/book}id']
# or
book_id = book.get('{http://example.com/book}id')
```

To set the value of an attribute, you can use the `set` method. For example, to set the value of the `id` attribute of the `book` element to `'bk103'`, you can write:

```
book.set('{http://example.com/book}id', 'bk103')
```

To find a child element by its tag name, you can use the `find` method. For example, to find the `bk:title` element of the `book` element, you can write:

```
title = book.find('{http://example.com/book}title')
```

To find all child elements by their tag name, you can use the `findall` method. For example, to find all the `book` elements of the `catalog` element, you can write:

```
books = catalog.findall('book')
```

To iterate over all child elements by their tag name, you can use the `iterfind` method. For example, to iterate over all the `book` elements of the `catalog` element, you can write:

```
for book in catalog.iterfind('book'):
    # do something with book
```

To iterate over all descendant elements by their tag name, you can use the `iter` method. For example, to iterate over all the elements with the `bk` namespace of the `catalog` element, you can write:

```
for element in catalog.iter('{http://example.com/book}*'):
    # do something with element
```

To add a new child element to an element, you can use the `append` or `insert` method. For example, to add a new `bk:rating` element to the `book` element, you can write:

```
rating = etree.Element('{http://example.com/book}rating')
rating.text = '4.5'
book.append(rating)
# or
book.insert(0, rating)
```

To remove a child element from an element, you can use the `remove` method. For example, to remove the `bk:price` element from the `book` element, you can write:

```
price = book.find('{http://example.com/book}price')
book.remove(price)
```

To remove all the attributes and child elements from an element, you can use the `clear` method. For example, to clear the `book` element, you can write:

```
book.clear()
```

## Validating and Transforming XML Data using Schemas and XSLT

To validate and transform XML data using schemas and XSLT in Python, you can use the `XMLSchema` and `XSLT` classes from lxml. The `XMLSchema` class takes an `ElementTree` object that represents an XML schema file, and provides methods such as `validate` and `assertValid` to check whether an XML data conforms to the schema. The `XSLT` class takes an `ElementTree` object that represents an XSLT file, and provides methods such as `apply` and `__call__` to transform an XML data using the XSLT.

For example, to validate the XML file `books.xml` against the XML schema file `books.xsd`, and to transform it using the XSLT file `books.xsl`, you can write:

```
from lxml import etree
tree = etree.parse('books.xml')
schema_tree = etree.parse('books.xsd')
schema = etree.XMLSchema(schema_tree)
schema.validate(tree) # returns True or False
schema.assertValid(tree) # raises an exception if invalid
xslt_tree = etree.parse('books.xsl')
```

```
xslt = etree.XSLT(xslt_tree)
result_tree = xslt(tree) # returns a new ElementTree object
result_tree.write('books.html', encoding='UTF-8',
pretty_print=True)
```

The XML schema file `books.xsd` could look something like this:

```
<?xml version="1.0" encoding="UTF-8"?>
<xs:schema xmlns:xs="http://www.w3.org/2001/XMLSchema"
           xmlns:bk="http://example.com/book"
           targetNamespace="http://example.com/book"
           elementFormDefault="qualified">
  <xs:element name="catalog">
    <xs:complexType>
      <xs:sequence>
        <xs:element name="book" maxOccurs="unbounded">
          <xs:complexType>
            <xs:sequence>
              <xs:element name="title" type="xs:string"/>
              <xs:element name="author" type="xs:string"/>
              <xs:element name="genre" type="xs:string"/>
              <xs:element name="price" type="xs:decimal"/>
              <xs:element name="publish_date"
type="xs:date"/>
              <xs:element name="description"
type="xs:string"/>
            </xs:sequence>
            <xs:attribute name="id" type="xs:string"
use="required"/>
          </xs:complexType>
        </xs:element>
      </xs:sequence>
    </xs:complexType>
  </xs:element>
</xs:schema>
```

The XSLT file `books.xsl` could look something like this:

```
<?xml version="1.0" encoding="UTF-8"?>
<xsl:stylesheet version="1.0"
xmlns:xsl="http://www.w3.org/1999/XSL/Transform"
                xmlns:bk="http://example.com/book">
  <xsl:output method="html" indent="yes"/>
  <xsl:template match="/">
    <html>
      <head>
        <title>Books Catalog</title>
```

```
      </head>
      <body>
        <h1>Books Catalog</h1>
        <table border="1">
          <tr>
            <th>Title</th>
            <th>Author</th>
            <th>Genre</th>
            <th>Price</th>
            <th>Publish Date</th>
            <th>Description</th>
          </tr>
          <xsl:for-each select="bk:catalog/bk:book">
            <tr>
              <td><xsl:value-of select="bk:title"/></td>
              <td><xsl:value-of select="bk:author"/></td>
              <td><xsl:value-of select="bk:genre"/></td>
              <td><xsl:value-of select="bk:price"/></td>
              <td><xsl:value-of
select="bk:publish_date"/></td>
              <td><xsl:value-of
select="bk:description"/></td>
            </tr>
          </xsl:for-each>
        </table>
      </body>
    </html>
  </xsl:template>
</xsl:stylesheet>
```

The result of applying the XSLT to the XML data would be an HTML file `books.html`, which would look something like this:

```
html
<html>
  <head>
    <meta http-equiv="Content-Type" content="text/html;
charset=UTF-8">
    <title>Books Catalog</title>
  </head>
  <body>
    <h1>Books Catalog</h1>
    <table border="1">
      <tr>
        <th>Title</th>
        <th>Author</th>
```

```
        <th>Genre</th>
        <th>Price</th>
        <th>Publish Date</th>
        <th>Description</th>
      </tr>
      <tr>
        <td>Python Developer's Guide</td>
        <td>Gambardella, Matthew</td>
        <td>Computer</td>
        <td>44.95</td>
        <td>2000-10-01</td>
        <td>An in-depth look at creating applications with 
Python.</td>
      </tr>
      <tr>
        <td>Midnight Rain</td>
        <td>Ralls, Kim</td>
        <td>Fantasy</td>
        <td>5.95</td>
        <td>2000-12-16</td>
        <td>A former architect battles corporate zombies, an 
evil sorceress, and her own childhood to become queen of the 
world.</td>
      </tr>
    </table>
  </body>
</html>
```

# Database

## Understanding SQL: The Language of Databases

SQL, or Structured Query Language, is the standard language for interacting with relational databases. It allows you to create, read, update, and delete (CRUD) data within a database. Below, we'll explore the fundamental SQL commands through practical examples.

## Creating Tables

To store data, we first need to create a table with a defined structure.

```
CREATE TABLE customers (
    customer_id INT PRIMARY KEY,
    name VARCHAR(100),
    email VARCHAR(100),
    join_date DATE
);
```

This SQL command creates a new table called `customers` with columns for the customer ID, name, email, and join date.

## Fetching Data

Once we have data, we can retrieve it using the `SELECT` statement.

```
SELECT * FROM customers;
```

This command fetches all columns (`*`) from the `customers` table.

## Inserting Data

To add new records to a table, we use the `INSERT INTO` command.

```
INSERT INTO customers (customer_id, name, email, join_date)
VALUES (1, 'Alice Smith', 'alice@example.com', '2021-07-03');
```

This inserts a new row with the specified values into the `customers` table.

# Updating Data

To modify existing data, the `UPDATE` statement is used.

```
UPDATE customers
SET email = 'alice.smith@example.com'
WHERE customer_id = 1;
```

This updates the email address for the customer with ID 1.

# Deleting Data

To remove data, the `DELETE` statement comes into play.

```
DELETE FROM customers
WHERE customer_id = 1;
```

This deletes the record of the customer with ID 1 from the `customers` table.

# Advanced Operations

SQL also supports more complex operations like joins and subqueries.

## Joins

Joins allow you to combine rows from two or more tables based on a related column.

```
SELECT orders.order_id, customers.name
FROM orders
INNER JOIN customers ON orders.customer_id =
customers.customer_id;
```

This retrieves order IDs and customer names by joining the `orders` and `customers` tables on the customer ID.

## Subqueries

Subqueries are queries nested within another SQL query.

```
SELECT name
FROM customers
WHERE customer_id IN (SELECT customer_id FROM orders WHERE
total > 100);
```

This fetches the names of customers who have placed orders totaling more than $100.

# SQL with Python

SQL data types define the kind of data that can be stored in a table column. When using SQL with Python, you typically interact with databases using libraries such as `sqlite3` for SQLite databases or `SQLAlchemy` for a more ORM-like approach that can interact with various database systems.

## SQL Data Types

- **INT**: For integer numbers.
- **VARCHAR(length)**: For variable-length strings.
- **TEXT**: For long-form text data.
- **DATE**: For date values (YYYY-MM-DD).
- **FLOAT**: For floating-point numbers.
- **BOOLEAN**: For true/false values.

## SQL Commands in Python

Here are some basic SQL commands and how you might use them in Python with the `sqlite3` library:

### Creating a Table

```
import sqlite3

# Connect to the database
conn = sqlite3.connect('example.db')
cursor = conn.cursor()

# Create a table
cursor.execute('''
CREATE TABLE users (
    id INT PRIMARY KEY,
    username VARCHAR(100),
    join_date DATE
)
''')
conn.commit()
```

### Inserting Data

```
# Insert data into the table
cursor.execute('''
INSERT INTO users (id, username, join_date) VALUES (?, ?, ?)
''', (1, 'john_doe', '2021-01-01'))
conn.commit()
```

### Querying Data

```
# Query data from the table
cursor.execute('SELECT * FROM users')
rows = cursor.fetchall()
for row in rows:
    print(row)
```

### Updating Data

```
# Update data in the table
cursor.execute('''
UPDATE users SET username = ? WHERE id = ?
''', ('jane_doe', 1))
conn.commit()
```

### Deleting Data

```
# Delete data from the table
cursor.execute('DELETE FROM users WHERE id = ?', (1,))
conn.commit()
```

After performing your database operations, don't forget to close the connection:

```
conn.close()
```

## Database Relationships

Creating relationships between tables is a core concept in SQL that allows you to link data across different tables. Below are the different types of relationships and how to implement them in Python:

### One-to-One Relationship

In a one-to-one relationship, each row in one table is linked to one and only one row in another table. This is often used for extending a table where one part rarely changes and the other part changes more frequently.

```
CREATE TABLE User (
    UserID int PRIMARY KEY,
    Username varchar(255) NOT NULL
);

CREATE TABLE UserProfile (
    UserID int PRIMARY KEY,
    DateOfBirth date NOT NULL,
    FOREIGN KEY (UserID) REFERENCES User(UserID)
);
```

### One-to-Many Relationship

A one-to-many relationship is where a row in one table can be related to many rows in another table. This is the most common relationship type.

```
CREATE TABLE Author (
    AuthorID int PRIMARY KEY,
    Name varchar(255) NOT NULL
);

CREATE TABLE Book (
    BookID int PRIMARY KEY,
    Title varchar(255) NOT NULL,
    AuthorID int,
    FOREIGN KEY (AuthorID) REFERENCES Author(AuthorID)
);
```

### Many-to-Many Relationship

In a many-to-many relationship, rows in one table can relate to multiple rows in another table, and vice versa. This usually requires a junction table.

```
CREATE TABLE Student (
    StudentID int PRIMARY KEY,
    StudentName varchar(255) NOT NULL
);

CREATE TABLE Course (
    CourseID int PRIMARY KEY,
    CourseName varchar(255) NOT NULL
);

CREATE TABLE Enrollment (
    StudentID int,
    CourseID int,
    PRIMARY KEY (StudentID, CourseID),
```

```
    FOREIGN KEY (StudentID) REFERENCES Student(StudentID),
    FOREIGN KEY (CourseID) REFERENCES Course(CourseID)
);
```

### Inserting Data

```
import sqlite3

# Connect to the database
conn = sqlite3.connect('example.db')
cursor = conn.cursor()

# Insert data into the Author table
cursor.execute("INSERT INTO Author (AuthorID, Name) VALUES
(?, ?)", (1, 'John Doe'))

# Commit the transaction
conn.commit()
```

### Updating Data

```
# Update data in the Book table
cursor.execute("UPDATE Book SET Title = ? WHERE BookID = ?",
('New Book Title', 1))

# Commit the transaction
conn.commit()

# Close the connection
conn.close()
```

### Self-Referencing Relationship

A self-referencing relationship is when a table has a foreign key that points to a primary key within the same table. This is often used for hierarchical data, such as an organizational structure where an employee reports to another employee.

For Example:

```
import sqlite3

# Connect to the SQLite database
conn = sqlite3.connect('company.db')
```

```
# Create a cursor object
cursor = conn.cursor()

# Create a table with a self-referencing foreign key
cursor.execute('''
CREATE TABLE employees (
    id INTEGER PRIMARY KEY,
    name TEXT NOT NULL,
    manager_id INTEGER,
    FOREIGN KEY (manager_id) REFERENCES employees(id)
)
''')

# Insert data into the table
# First, insert the top-level employee (e.g., CEO) who has no
manager
cursor.execute("INSERT INTO employees (name, manager_id)
VALUES (?, ?)", ('CEO', None))

# Save (commit) the changes
conn.commit()

# Now, insert an employee with a manager
# Assuming the CEO has an ID of 1
cursor.execute("INSERT INTO employees (name, manager_id)
VALUES (?, ?)", ('Manager', 1))

# Save (commit) the changes
conn.commit()

# Close the connection
conn.close()
```

In this example, the `employees` table has a column `manager_id` that references the `id` column within the same table, creating a self-referencing relationship. The CEO is inserted first with a `NULL` `manager_id`, and then a manager is inserted with the CEO's `id` as their `manager_id`.

**Many-to-One Relationship**

A many-to-one relationship occurs when multiple records in one table reference a single record in another table.

For Example:

```
# Create two tables: authors and books
# Each book references an author
```

```
cursor.execute('''
CREATE TABLE authors (
    id INTEGER PRIMARY KEY,
    name TEXT NOT NULL
)
''')

cursor.execute('''
CREATE TABLE books (
    id INTEGER PRIMARY KEY,
    title TEXT NOT NULL,
    author_id INTEGER,
    FOREIGN KEY (author_id) REFERENCES authors(id)
)
''')

# Commit the changes
conn.commit()
```

## Inserting Data

```
# Insert an author
cursor.execute("INSERT INTO authors (name) VALUES (?)",
('Author Name',))

# Insert a book
cursor.execute("INSERT INTO books (title, author_id) VALUES
(?, ?)", ('Book Title', 1))

# Commit the changes
conn.commit()
```

## Updating Data

```
# Update an author's name
cursor.execute("UPDATE authors SET name = ? WHERE id = ?",
('New Author Name', 1))

# Update a book's title
cursor.execute("UPDATE books SET title = ? WHERE id = ?",
('New Book Title', 1))

# Commit the changes
conn.commit()
```

After performing your database operations, don't forget to close the connection:

```
conn.close()
```

## Security

Protecting your application from SQL injection attacks is crucial for maintaining data integrity and security. Here's a guide with code examples to help you safeguard your applications:

### Use Parameterized Queries

Parameterized queries ensure that the SQL engine recognizes the code and data separately, preventing attackers from injecting malicious SQL.

**Example with sqlite3:**

```
import sqlite3

# Connect to the database
conn = sqlite3.connect('database.db')

# Create a cursor object
cursor = conn.cursor()

# Safe parameterized query
user_id = 'example_user_id'
cursor.execute("SELECT * FROM users WHERE id = ?",
(user_id,))
```

### Use ORM Frameworks

Object-Relational Mapping (ORM) frameworks like SQLAlchemy in Python or Entity Framework in .NET can abstract SQL code and prevent injections.

**Example with SQLAlchemy:**

```
from sqlalchemy import create_engine, text

# Create an engine
engine = create_engine('sqlite:///database.db')

# Safe query with SQLAlchemy
user_id = 'example_user_id'
with engine.connect() as conn:
```

```
    result = conn.execute(text("SELECT * FROM users WHERE id
= :user_id"), {'user_id': user_id})
```

**Input Validation**

Validate user input against a set of rules (e.g., type, length, format) before including it in SQL queries.

```
user_input = 'example_user_id'

# Simple validation check
if not user_input.isalnum():
    raise ValueError("Invalid input")
```

# Excel File

## Reading Data from Excel Files

Python provides powerful libraries such as `pandas` and `openpyxl` to read data from Excel files. Here's how you can use them:

### Using pandas

```
import pandas as pd

# Load an Excel file into a pandas DataFrame
df = pd.read_excel('path_to_file.xlsx')

# Display the first few rows of the DataFrame
print(df.head())
```

### Using openpyxl

```
from openpyxl import load_workbook

# Load the workbook and select the active worksheet
wb = load_workbook('path_to_file.xlsx')
sheet = wb.active

# Read data from the worksheet
data = []
for row in sheet.iter_rows(values_only=True):
    data.append(row)

# Print the data
for row in data:
    print(row)
```

## Writing Data to Excel Files

Writing data back to Excel files is just as straightforward:

### Using pandas

```
# Assuming 'df' is a pandas DataFrame with your data

# Write the DataFrame to an Excel file
df.to_excel('output.xlsx', index=False)
```

### Using openpyxl

```
from openpyxl import Workbook

# Create a new workbook and select the active worksheet
wb = Workbook()
sheet = wb.active

# Assuming 'data' is a list of tuples with your data
for row in data:
    sheet.append(row)

# Save the workbook
wb.save('output.xlsx')
```

## pandas vs openpyxl

When choosing between `pandas` and `openpyxl`, consider the following:

**Advantages of pandas:**

- Simplified syntax for reading and writing.
- Integrated data manipulation capabilities.
- Better performance with large datasets.

**Disadvantages of pandas:**

- Less control over specific Excel features.
- Heavier dependency due to its extensive functionality.

**Advantages of openpyxl:**

- Fine-grained control over Excel file components.
- Ability to handle Excel-specific features like formulas and charts.

**Disadvantages of openpyxl:**

- More verbose code for simple read/write operations.
- Potentially slower with large datasets.

## Data Manipulation During I/O

Filtering, sorting, and pivoting data with `pandas`:

```
import pandas as pd

# Read the Excel file
df = pd.read_excel('sales_data.xlsx')

# Filter rows where sales are greater than $500
filtered_df = df[df['Sales'] > 500]

# Sort the DataFrame by the 'Sales' column
sorted_df = filtered_df.sort_values(by='Sales',
ascending=False)

# Pivot the data by product category
pivot_df = pd.pivot_table(df, index='Category',
values='Sales', aggfunc='sum')

# Write the manipulated data back to an Excel file
pivot_df.to_excel('manipulated_sales_data.xlsx')
```

# Parallel Processing

Parallelism in computing refers to the practice of performing multiple calculations or tasks simultaneously to increase computational speed and efficiency. This concept is based on the idea that large problems can often be divided into smaller ones, which can then be solved at the same time.

## Advantages of Parallel Computing

- **Speed**: Parallel computing can significantly reduce the time required to solve complex problems by dividing the workload across multiple processors.
- **Cost-Effectiveness**: It can be more cost-effective as it allows for the use of multiple cheaper processing units instead of a single, more expensive unit.
- **Solving Larger Problems**: Some problems are too large to solve on a single CPU, and parallel computing makes it feasible to tackle them.
- **Efficient Use of Resources**: It allows for the full utilization of computational resources, as multiple processors can work on different parts of a problem simultaneously.

## Use Cases for Parallelism

- **High-Performance Computing**: Used in scientific research and engineering to perform large-scale simulations and calculations.
- **Graphics Rendering**: Used in graphics and video rendering to process multiple pixels or frames at the same time.
- **Big Data Analysis**: Used to process and analyze large datasets more quickly.
- **Real-Time Processing**: Used in systems that require real-time data processing, such as autonomous vehicles and financial trading systems.

Parallel computing is closely related to concurrent computing, but they are distinct concepts. Concurrency involves multiple sequences of operations happening in overlapping time periods, which doesn't mean they are happening at the exact same moment, as with parallelism.

Parallelism in Python can be implemented in several ways, each with its own use cases and advantages. Here are some of the key methods:

- **Multiprocessing**: This is a package that supports spawning processes using an API similar to the threading module. It allows you to create multiple processes, each running its own instance of the Python interpreter. This is useful for CPU-bound tasks and bypasses the Global Interpreter Lock (GIL) that can limit the performance of threaded applications.
- **Threading**: Despite the GIL, threading can be useful for I/O-bound tasks. Threads run in the same memory space, which means they're lightweight and have low memory overhead compared to processes.
- **Concurrent.Futures**: This is a high-level interface for asynchronously executing callables. The asynchronous execution can be performed with threads, using `ThreadPoolExecutor`, or separate processes, using `ProcessPoolExecutor`.
- **Asyncio**: This is a library to write concurrent code using the async/await syntax. It's suitable for single-threaded concurrent code that handles many connections or other I/O-bound tasks.

Each method has its own best practices and scenarios where it excels. For example, `multiprocessing` is great for CPU-intensive tasks, while `asyncio` shines in handling large numbers of I/O operations concurrently.

# Multiprocessing

Multiprocessing in Python is a powerful feature that allows you to create programs that can run multiple processes simultaneously. This is particularly useful for CPU-bound tasks where you want to make use of multiple CPU cores. Here's a deeper look into how multiprocessing works in Python:

**Process Creation and Management:**

- **Process Class**: You create a new process by instantiating the `Process` class with a target function and its arguments.
- **Start and Join**: To start the process, you call its `start()` method. After starting all processes, you call `join()` to ensure that the parent process

waits for all child processes to complete.

**Example of Creating and Running a Process:**

```
from multiprocessing import Process

def f(name):
    print('hello', name)

if __name__ == '__main__':
    p = Process(target=f, args=('Bob',))
    p.start()
    p.join()
```

**Data Parallelism with Pool:**

- **Pool Object**: The `Pool` class is used for parallelizing the execution of a function across multiple input values.
- **Map Method**: The `map()` method of the `Pool` object maps a function to an iterable and executes them in parallel.

**Example of Using Pool:**

```
from multiprocessing import Pool

def f(x):
    return x*x

if __name__ == '__main__':
    with Pool(5) as p:
        print(p.map(f, [1, 2, 3]))
```

**Contexts and Start Methods:**

- **Contexts**: Depending on the platform, multiprocessing supports different ways to start a process, such as `spawn`, `fork`, and `forkserver`.
- **Start Methods**: The `spawn` method starts a fresh Python interpreter process, which is the default on Windows and macOS.

**Best Practices:**

- **Use Context Managers**: To manage resources efficiently, use context managers with `Pool`.
- **Main Module Idiom**: Always guard the entry point of the multiprocessing

program with `if __name__ == '__main__':` to ensure proper behavior.

**Common Issues:**

- **Global Interpreter Lock (GIL)**: Multiprocessing bypasses the GIL by creating separate processes instead of threads, allowing full utilization of multiple processors.
- **Sharing State**: Processes have separate memory spaces, so sharing state between them requires using shared memory objects or server processes.

## Multiprocessing use-cases

**1. Data Processing:** When dealing with large datasets, you can use multiprocessing to distribute data processing tasks across multiple processes. This is particularly useful when the tasks are CPU-intensive and can be performed independently.

**Example:**

```
from multiprocessing import Pool

def process_data(data_chunk):
    # Process data
    return processed_data

if __name__ == '__main__':
    dataset = get_large_dataset()
    with Pool(processes=4) as pool:
        results = pool.map(process_data, dataset)
```

**2. Web Server:** In a web server, you might use multiprocessing to handle multiple requests simultaneously, ensuring that each request is processed independently without blocking others.

**Example:**

```
from multiprocessing import Process
from my_web_server import handle_request

def serve_forever(port):
    while True:
        request = get_request(port)
        p = Process(target=handle_request, args=(request,))
        p.start()
```

```
if __name__ == '__main__':
    serve_forever(80)
```

**3. Scientific Computing:** For scientific computations that require heavy CPU usage, multiprocessing can be used to parallelize complex calculations across multiple cores.

**Example:**

```
from multiprocessing import Pool

def compute_complex_operation(x):
    # Complex computation
    return x * x

if __name__ == '__main__':
    inputs = range(1000000)
    with Pool() as pool:
        results = pool.map(compute_complex_operation, inputs)
```

**4. Real-time Data Analysis:** In scenarios where you need to analyze data in real-time, such as stock market analysis, multiprocessing can help to process incoming data streams in parallel.

**Example:**

```
from multiprocessing import Process, Queue

def data_analyzer(queue):
    while True:
        data = queue.get()
        analyze_data(data)

if __name__ == '__main__':
    data_queue = Queue()
    p = Process(target=data_analyzer, args=(data_queue,))
    p.start()

    while True:
        # Get real-time data
        data_queue.put(new_data)
```

**5. Image Processing:** Multiprocessing can significantly speed up image processing tasks by dividing the workload across multiple processors.

**Example:**

```
from multiprocessing import Pool

def process_image(image):
    # Image processing
    return processed_image

if __name__ == '__main__':
    images = load_images()
    with Pool() as pool:
        processed_images = pool.map(process_image, images)
```

In each of these scenarios, the key is to identify the parts of your program that can be executed in parallel and to design your multiprocessing setup accordingly. It's also important to handle the communication between processes carefully, especially when it comes to sharing data.

## Memory management in multiprocessing

Memory management in Python's multiprocessing is a critical aspect, as each process has its own memory space. Here are some practical examples and scenarios that illustrate how to manage memory in multiprocessing:

**Shared Memory:** When you want to share data between processes, you can use shared memory. The `multiprocessing` module provides `Value` and `Array` types for sharing data.

**Example of Shared Memory:**

```
from multiprocessing import Process, Value, Array

def f(n, a):
    n.value = 3.1415927
    for i in range(len(a)):
        a[i] = -a[i]

if __name__ == '__main__':
    num = Value('d', 0.0)
    arr = Array('i', range(10))

    p = Process(target=f, args=(num, arr))
    p.start()
    p.join()

    print(num.value)
    print(arr[:])
```

**Server Process:** For more complex data or when you need to support arbitrary object types, you can use a manager server process that holds Python objects and allows other processes to manipulate them using proxies.

**Example of Server Process:**

```
from multiprocessing import Process, Manager

def f(d, l):
    d[1] = '1'
    d['2'] = 2
    d[0.25] = None
    l.reverse()

if __name__ == '__main__':
    with Manager() as manager:
        d = manager.dict()
        l = manager.list(range(10))

        p = Process(target=f, args=(d, l))
        p.start()
        p.join()

        print(d)
        print(l)
```

**Synchronization:** When multiple processes need to access the same data, synchronization mechanisms like locks can prevent data corruption.

**Example of Synchronization:**

```
from multiprocessing import Process, Lock, Value

def f(l, v):
    with l:
        v.value += 1

if __name__ == '__main__':
    lock = Lock()
    v = Value('i', 0)

    processes = [Process(target=f, args=(lock, v)) for i in
range(10)]

    for p in processes:
        p.start()
```

```
    for p in processes:
        p.join()

    print(v.value)
```

**Shared Memory Blocks:** For sharing large blocks of data, you can use the `shared_memory` module introduced in Python 3.8.

**Example of Shared Memory Blocks:**

```
from multiprocessing import shared_memory
from multiprocessing import Process
import array

# Create a shared memory block
shm = shared_memory.SharedMemory(create=True, size=10)
# Create an array of integers using the shared memory block
# Write the data to shared memory
shm.buf[0] = 0

# Access the shared memory in another process
def access_shared_memory(shm_name, value):
    existing_shm = shared_memory.SharedMemory(name=shm_name)
    # Read the data from shared memory
    print(f"{value} process",)
    existing_shm.buf[0] += value
    existing_shm.close()

processes = [Process(target=access_shared_memory,
args=(shm.name, i)) for i in range(10)]

for p in processes:
    p.start()

for p in processes:
    p.join()

print("Final result",shm.buf[0])
# Clean up shared memory
shm.close()
shm.unlink()
```

These examples demonstrate different ways to manage memory across processes in Python. It's important to choose the right approach based on the requirements of your application, such as the type of data being shared, the size of the data, and the level of complexity you're willing to manage.

## Generators for Multiprocessing

Using generators for parallel processing in Python can be achieved by combining them with the `multiprocessing` module, which allows different parts of your program to run concurrently. This can be particularly useful when you want to perform CPU-intensive tasks on large datasets.

Here's a basic example of how you might use a generator with the `multiprocessing` module:

```
import multiprocessing

# Define a generator function
def data_stream():
    for data in range(10):  # Replace this with your actual
data source
        yield data

# Define a function to process data
def process_data(data):
    print(f"Processing {data}")
    # Your data processing logic here

if __name__ == "__main__":
    pool = multiprocessing.Pool(multiprocessing.cpu_count())
    for data in data_stream():
        pool.apply_async(process_data, args=(data,))
    pool.close()
    pool.join()
```

In this example:

- `data_stream` is a generator function that yields data items.
- `process_data` is the function that will process each item of data.
- We create a pool of worker processes equal to the number of CPUs available.
- We use `apply_async` to process each data item asynchronously.

This setup allows each item from the generator to be processed in parallel by different worker processes. The `apply_async` method schedules the `process_data` function to be executed with the data as soon as a worker process is available.

# Threading

A thread is a separate flow of execution within a process. Unlike multiprocessing, threads run in the same memory space, allowing them to share data more easily. However, because of the Global Interpreter Lock (GIL) in CPython, threads may not run truly in parallel but are rather interleaved, which can be beneficial for I/O-bound tasks.

### Creating Threads

You can create threads using the `threading` module in Python.

**Example:**

```
import threading

def print_numbers():
    for i in range(5):
        print(i)

# Create a thread
t = threading.Thread(target=print_numbers)
# Start the thread
t.start()
# Wait for the thread to complete
t.join()
```

### Daemon Threads

Daemon threads are background threads that automatically exit when all non-daemon threads have completed. They are set by passing `daemon=True` to the `Thread` constructor or calling `setDaemon(True)` on the thread object.

**Synchronization:** To avoid race conditions, Python provides synchronization primitives like `Lock`, `RLock`, `Semaphore`, `Event`, and `Condition`.

**Example of Using a Lock:**

```
import threading

lock = threading.Lock()

def safe_print(item):
    with lock:
```

```
        print(item)

threads = [threading.Thread(target=safe_print, args=(i,)) for
i in range(5)]

for t in threads:
    t.start()
for t in threads:
    t.join()
```

### ThreadPoolExecutor

For managing a pool of threads, you can use `ThreadPoolExecutor`.

**Example:**

```
from concurrent.futures import ThreadPoolExecutor

def task(n):
    print(f"Processing {n}")

with ThreadPoolExecutor(max_workers=3) as executor:
    for i in range(5):
        executor.submit(task, i)
```

**Common Issues:**

- **GIL**: The GIL can make it difficult to achieve true parallelism in CPU-bound tasks.
- **Race Conditions**: When threads share mutable data, they can interfere with each other, leading to inconsistent results.

**Best Practices:**

- **Use `Queue`**: For thread-safe data exchange.
- **Avoid Global State**: Minimize shared state between threads.
- **Profile First**: Determine if threading will actually benefit your program.

Here's how you can set up a system where a generator produces items that are then consumed by multiple worker processes through a queue.

**Step 1: Create a Generator**
First, you need a generator function that yields items to be processed. This could be data read from a file, generated on-the-fly, or fetched from an API.

```
def data_generator():
    for data in range(100):  # Replace with your data source
        yield data
```

**Step 2: Set Up a Queue**

You can use the `Queue` class from Python's `queue` module to create a queue that will hold the items to be processed.

```
from queue import Queue

# Create a FIFO queue
data_queue = Queue(maxsize=10)  # maxsize is optional
```

**Step 3: Populate the Queue**

You can have a dedicated thread or process that takes items from the generator and puts them into the queue.

```
def producer(queue, generator):
    for item in generator:
        queue.put(item)  # Blocks if the queue is full
```

**Step 4: Create Worker Processes**

Set up worker processes that will consume items from the queue and process them. You can use the `multiprocessing` module for this.

```
from multiprocessing import Process

def worker(queue):
    while True:
        item = queue.get()  # Blocks until an item is
available
        if item is None:  # Use 'None' as a signal to stop
            break
        process_data(item)  # Replace with your processing
logic
        queue.task_done()
```

**Step 5: Start the System**

Finally, you start the producer and worker processes and let them run.

```
# Start the producer thread
producer_thread = threading.Thread(target=producer,
args=(data_queue, data_generator()))
producer_thread.start()
```

```
# Start worker processes
num_workers = 4  # Number of workers
workers = []
for _ in range(num_workers):
    p = Process(target=worker, args=(data_queue,))
    p.start()
    workers.append(p)

# Wait for the producer to finish
producer_thread.join()

# Signal the workers to stop
for _ in range(num_workers):
    data_queue.put(None)

# Wait for all workers to finish
for p in workers:
    p.join()
```

**Complete code:**

```
# Wait for all workers to finish
from multiprocessing import Process
from queue import Queue
import threading

def data_generator():
    for data in range(100):  # Replace with your data source
        yield data
# Create a FIFO queue
data_queue = Queue(maxsize=10)  # maxsize is optional

def producer(queue, generator):
    for item in generator:
        queue.put(item)  # Blocks if the queue is full
def process_data(item):
    print(item)
def worker(queue):
    while True:
        item = queue.get()  # Blocks until an item is
available
        if item is None:  # Use 'None' as a signal to stop
            break
        process_data(item)  # Replace with your processing
logic
        queue.task_done()
```

```
# Start the producer thread
producer_thread = threading.Thread(target=producer,
args=(data_queue, data_generator()))
producer_thread.start()

# Start worker processes
num_workers = 4  # Number of workers
workers = []
for _ in range(num_workers):
    p = Process(target=worker, args=(data_queue,))
    p.start()
    workers.append(p)

# Wait for the producer to finish
producer_thread.join()

# Signal the workers to stop
for _ in range(num_workers):
    data_queue.put(None)

# Wait for all workers to finish
for p in workers:
    p.join()
```

In this setup, the producer thread reads data from the generator and puts it into the queue. The worker processes take items from the queue and process them. When the producer is done, it puts `None` into the queue for each worker as a signal to stop.

## Thread Safety

Thread safety is a concept in the context of multi-threading, where multiple threads are executing code simultaneously. An operation or piece of code is considered thread-safe if it functions correctly during simultaneous execution by multiple threads. This means that shared data accessed by threads are protected from race conditions and other concurrency issues that could lead to inconsistent or incorrect behavior.

To ensure thread safety, you can use synchronization mechanisms provided by the `threading` module, such as:

- **Locks**: A Lock can be used to ensure that only one thread can access a particular piece of code at a time.
- **RLocks (Reentrant Locks)**: These are locks that can be acquired multiple

times by the same thread.

- **Semaphores**: A semaphore restricts access to a limited number of threads.
- **Events**: An event is a synchronization primitive that can be used to manage the state within threads.
- **Conditions**: These are used for signaling between threads, allowing one thread to pause until notified by another.
- **Queues**: The `queue` module provides a thread-safe FIFO implementation.

Here's an example using a Lock to ensure that only one thread can increment a counter at a time:

```
import threading

class ThreadSafeCounter:
    def __init__(self):
        self.counter = 0
        self.lock = threading.Lock()

    def increment(self):
        with self.lock:
            self.counter += 1

# Create a thread-safe counter
counter = ThreadSafeCounter()

# Function to increment the counter
def increment_counter():
    for _ in range(1000):
        counter.increment()

# Create threads to increment the counter
threads = [threading.Thread(target=increment_counter) for _
in range(10)]

# Start threads
for thread in threads:
    thread.start()

# Wait for all threads to complete
for thread in threads:
    thread.join()
```

```
print(f"Counter value: {counter.counter}")
```

In this example, the `increment` method of `ThreadSafeCounter` uses a `Lock` to ensure that the `counter` variable is only modified by one thread at a time, preventing race conditions.

Let's explore various synchronization mechanisms provided by Python's `threading` module and the scenarios where they might be implemented:

**Lock**

A Lock is used when you want to ensure that only one thread can access a particular resource at a time. It's the most basic synchronization primitive.

Imagine a scenario where multiple threads are writing to a single file. To prevent data corruption, you would use a Lock to ensure that only one thread can write to the file at a time.

```
import threading

file_lock = threading.Lock()

def write_to_file(data):
    with file_lock:
        # Critical section of code to write data to a file
        pass
```

**RLock (Reentrant Lock)**

An RLock allows a thread that has acquired it to acquire it again without blocking, which is useful in recursive functions.

Consider a recursive function that needs to acquire a lock before proceeding. An RLock will allow the same thread to acquire the lock multiple times without deadlocking.

```
import threading

rlock = threading.RLock()

def recursive_function():
    with rlock:
        # The same thread can acquire the rlock again
        recursive_function()
```

### Semaphore

A Semaphore is used to limit the number of threads that can access a particular resource at a time.

If you have a pool of database connections and want to limit the number of concurrent accesses to the pool, you could use a Semaphore.

```
import threading

pool_semaphore = threading.Semaphore(10)

def access_database():
    with pool_semaphore:
        # Access the database connection pool
        pass
```

### Event

An Event is used for signaling between threads. One thread signals an event and other threads wait for it.

In a multi-threaded download manager, one thread might need to signal others that a download has completed before they can proceed with processing the downloaded data.

```
import threading

download_event = threading.Event()

def downloader():
    # Download logic here
    download_event.set()  # Signal that the download is
complete

def processor():
    download_event.wait()  # Wait for the download to
complete
    # Process the downloaded data
```

### Condition

A Condition is used when one thread needs to wait for a certain condition to be met before proceeding.

Imagine a producer-consumer problem where the consumer threads should wait until the producer has produced some items.

```
import threading

condition = threading.Condition()

def consumer():
    with condition:
        condition.wait()  # Wait for the condition to be met
        # Consume the item

def producer():
    with condition:
        # Produce an item
        condition.notify_all()  # Notify all waiting
consumers
```

### Queue

A Queue is a thread-safe FIFO data structure that is used for inter-thread communication.

In a web server, incoming HTTP requests could be placed in a Queue by one thread and processed by a pool of worker threads.

```
import queue

request_queue = queue.Queue()

def handle_requests():
    while True:
        request = request_queue.get()  # Get a request from
the queue
        # Handle the request
```

Each synchronization mechanism serves a specific purpose and can be chosen based on the requirements of the concurrent program you are developing. The examples provided illustrate how these mechanisms can be applied to common multi-threading problems.

# concurrent.futures

The `concurrent.futures` module in Python provides a high-level interface for asynchronously executing callables. It's part of the standard library and offers two main executor classes - `ThreadPoolExecutor` and `ProcessPoolExecutor` - which allow you to execute tasks concurrently using threads or processes, respectively.

Here's a detailed look into `concurrent.futures`:

**ThreadPoolExecutor:**

- Ideal for I/O-bound tasks where operations often wait for external resources.
- Uses a pool of threads to execute calls asynchronously.

Example of using `ThreadPoolExecutor` to perform tasks concurrently:

```
from concurrent.futures import ThreadPoolExecutor,
as_completed
import requests

def fetch_url(url):
    # Logic to fetch data from the URL
    data = requests.get(url)
    return data.status_code

urls = ['http://google.com', 'http://openai.com']
with ThreadPoolExecutor(max_workers=5) as executor:
    future_to_url = {executor.submit(fetch_url, url): url for
url in urls}
    for future in as_completed(future_to_url):
        url = future_to_url[future]
        try:
            data = future.result()
        except Exception as exc:
            print('%r generated an exception: %s' % (url,
exc))
        else:
            print('%r page is %d bytes' % (url, len(data)))
```

**ProcessPoolExecutor:**

- Suitable for CPU-bound tasks that require heavy computation.
- Uses a pool of processes to execute calls asynchronously, which can take

advantage of multiple CPU cores.

Example of using `ProcessPoolExecutor` to perform computationally intensive tasks concurrently:

```
from concurrent.futures import ProcessPoolExecutor

def compute_factorial(number):
    # Logic to compute factorial
    result = [number * i for i in range(100)]
    return result

numbers = [5, 7, 11]
with ProcessPoolExecutor() as executor:
    results = list(executor.map(compute_factorial, numbers))
```

**Key Features:**

- Both `ThreadPoolExecutor` and `ProcessPoolExecutor` implement the `Executor` interface, which provides methods like `submit()` and `map()`.
- The `submit()` method schedules a callable to be executed and returns a `Future` object representing the execution.
- The `map()` method is similar to the built-in `map()` function but executes the function calls asynchronously.

**Best Practices:**

- Use `ThreadPoolExecutor` for tasks that are waiting on I/O operations.
- Use `ProcessPoolExecutor` for tasks that are limited by CPU processing.
- Properly manage the executor's lifecycle using context managers to ensure resources are freed.

## ThreadPoolExecutor

The `ThreadPoolExecutor` is a component of the `concurrent.futures` module in Python that manages a pool of threads to execute function calls asynchronously. It provides an efficient way to handle concurrent execution of tasks, particularly for I/O-bound operations, where tasks can be performed in parallel without waiting for one another to complete.

### Creating a ThreadPoolExecutor

You create a `ThreadPoolExecutor` by specifying the maximum number of threads that can run simultaneously. It's common to use the `with` statement to ensure that resources are cleaned up promptly when the execution is done.

**Example:**

```
from concurrent.futures import ThreadPoolExecutor

# Create a ThreadPoolExecutor with a maximum of four worker
threads
with ThreadPoolExecutor(max_workers=4) as executor:
    # Tasks to be executed by the thread pool
    ...
```

### Submitting Tasks

You can submit tasks to the executor using the `submit()` method, which schedules a callable to be executed and returns a `Future` object.

**Example:**

```
def load_url(url, timeout):
    # Logic to load data from the URL
    return data

# Submit tasks to the executor
future = executor.submit(load_url, 'http://example.com', 60)
```

### Using the map Method

The `map()` method is used to apply a function to multiple inputs in parallel. Unlike the built-in `map()`, the `ThreadPoolExecutor`'s `map()` method returns results as soon as they are available.

**Example:**

```
urls = ['http://example.com', 'http://another.com']
results = executor.map(load_url, urls)
```

### Handling Future Objects

A `Future` object represents the eventual result of an asynchronous operation. You can check if a task is completed using `done()`, get the result with `result()`, or handle exceptions with `exception()`.

**Example:**

```
# Check if the task is completed
if future.done():
    try:
        # Get the result
        data = future.result()
    except Exception as exc:
        # Handle exceptions
        print(f'An exception occurred: {exc}')
```

### Shutting Down the Executor

It's important to shut down the executor when it's no longer needed. The `shutdown()` method frees up system resources. The `with` statement handles this automatically.

**Best Practices:**

- Use `ThreadPoolExecutor` for I/O-bound tasks.
- Avoid using it for CPU-bound tasks due to the Global Interpreter Lock (GIL).
- Manage the lifecycle of the executor properly to avoid resource leaks.

The `ThreadPoolExecutor` is a powerful tool for improving the performance of I/O-bound applications. It allows you to execute tasks concurrently, which can significantly reduce the overall execution time of your program.

### Thread Template

This class, named `TaskExecutor`, provides methods to submit tasks, retrieve results, and handle exceptions.

```
from concurrent.futures import ThreadPoolExecutor,
as_completed
import threading

class TaskExecutor:
    def __init__(self, max_workers=5):
        self.executor =
```

```
ThreadPoolExecutor(max_workers=max_workers)
        self.lock = threading.Lock()
        self.futures = []

    def submit_task(self, func, *args, **kwargs):
        future = self.executor.submit(func, *args, **kwargs)
        with self.lock:
            self.futures.append(future)
        return future

    def get_results(self):
        for future in as_completed(self.futures):
            try:
                yield future.result()
            except Exception as exc:
                yield exc

    def shutdown(self, wait=True):
        self.executor.shutdown(wait=wait)

# Example usage:
if __name__ == "__main__":
    def task_function(task_id):
        print(f"Executing task {task_id}")
        # Simulate task execution
        return f"Result of task {task_id}"

    # Create an instance of TaskExecutor
    executor = TaskExecutor(max_workers=3)

    # Submit tasks
    for i in range(10):
        executor.submit_task(task_function, i)

    # Retrieve and print results
    for result in executor.get_results():
        print(result)

    # Shutdown the executor
    executor.shutdown()
```

This `TaskExecutor` class provides a simple interface to submit tasks, collect results, and manage the lifecycle of the `ThreadPoolExecutor`. It also includes a lock to ensure thread safety when accessing the list of futures.

Remember to replace `task_function` and the loop where tasks are submitted with your actual task logic and inputs. This is just a template to demonstrate how you might structure such a class.

## ProcessPoolExecutor

The `ProcessPoolExecutor` is a feature in the `concurrent.futures` module of Python that provides a high-level interface for parallel execution of tasks across multiple processors. It is particularly useful for CPU-bound tasks that can be performed concurrently.

Here's a detailed look into `ProcessPoolExecutor`:

**Creating a ProcessPoolExecutor:** You instantiate a `ProcessPoolExecutor` with an optional argument `max_workers`, which specifies the number of worker processes to use. If `max_workers` is not specified, it defaults to the number of processors on the machine.

**Example:**

```
from concurrent.futures import ProcessPoolExecutor

# Create a ProcessPoolExecutor with a specific number of
worker processes
with ProcessPoolExecutor(max_workers=4) as executor:
    # Tasks to be executed by the process pool
    ...
```

### Submitting Tasks

Tasks are submitted to the executor using the `submit()` method, which schedules a callable to be executed and returns a `Future` object representing the execution of the callable.

**Example:**

```
def compute_some_function(data):
    # Computationally intensive operations
    return result

# Submit tasks to the executor
future = executor.submit(compute_some_function, data)
```

### Using the map Method

The `map()` method simplifies the process of submitting tasks. It applies a given function to every item of an iterable and returns an iterator that yields the results.

**Example:**

```
data_list = [data1, data2, data3]
results = executor.map(compute_some_function, data_list)
```

### Handling Future Objects

`Future` objects encapsulate the asynchronous execution of a callable and allow you to check on the status of the task, retrieve results, or handle exceptions.

**Example:**

```
# Check if the task is completed
if future.done():
    try:
        # Get the result
        result = future.result()
    except Exception as exc:
        # Handle exceptions
        print(f'An exception occurred: {exc}')
```

### Shutting Down the Executor

It's important to shut down the executor when it's no longer needed to free up system resources. The `shutdown()` method is called automatically when exiting the `with` block.

**Best Practices:**

- Use `ProcessPoolExecutor` for CPU-bound tasks that can run independently of each other.
- Be mindful of the number of worker processes to avoid overloading the system.
- Ensure that the tasks are independent and do not need to share extensive amounts of data, as inter-process communication can be costly.

The `ProcessPoolExecutor` is a powerful tool for speeding up CPU-intensive operations by taking advantage of multiple CPU cores and parallel processing.

## Process Template

This class, named `ParallelExecutor`, provides methods to submit tasks, retrieve results, and handle exceptions in a process pool.

```
from concurrent.futures import ProcessPoolExecutor,
as_completed
import multiprocessing

class ParallelExecutor:
    def __init__(self, max_workers=None):
        # If max_workers is None, the number of workers is
set to the number of CPU cores
        self.max_workers = max_workers or
multiprocessing.cpu_count()
        self.executor =
ProcessPoolExecutor(max_workers=self.max_workers)
        self.futures = []

    def submit_task(self, func, *args, **kwargs):
        # Submit a task to the process pool
        future = self.executor.submit(func, *args, **kwargs)
        self.futures.append(future)
        return future

    def get_results(self):
        # Yield results as they are completed
        for future in as_completed(self.futures):
            try:
                yield future.result()
            except Exception as exc:
                yield exc

    def shutdown(self, wait=True):
        # Shutdown the process pool
        self.executor.shutdown(wait=wait)

# Example usage:
if __name__ == "__main__":
    def compute_function(x):
        # A CPU-bound task, e.g., a complex computation
        return [x * i for i in range(10)]

    # Create an instance of ParallelExecutor
    executor = ParallelExecutor()

    # Submit tasks
```

```
    for i in range(10):
        executor.submit_task(compute_function, i)

    # Retrieve and print results
    for result in executor.get_results():
        print(result)

    # Shutdown the executor
    executor.shutdown()
```

This `ParallelExecutor` class allows you to easily manage a pool of processes for executing tasks in parallel. You can submit tasks to the pool and retrieve their results asynchronously. The `shutdown` method ensures that all processes are cleanly terminated.

# Asyncio

`Asyncio` is a library in Python that provides the infrastructure for writing single-threaded concurrent code using coroutines, multiplexing I/O access over sockets and other resources, running network clients and servers, and other related primitives. Here's a detailed look into `asyncio` and how it works:

**Key Concepts of Asyncio:**

- **Coroutines**: A coroutine is a function that can suspend its execution before reaching return, and it can indirectly pass control to another coroutine for some time. Coroutines are declared with the `async def` syntax.
- **Event Loop**: The event loop is the core of every asyncio application. It runs in a thread (typically the main thread) and executes all callbacks and tasks in its thread.
- **Tasks**: Tasks are used to schedule coroutines concurrently. When a coroutine is wrapped into a Task with functions like `asyncio.create_task()`, the coroutine is automatically scheduled to run soon.
- **Futures**: A Future is a special low-level awaitable object that represents an eventual result of an asynchronous operation. When a Future object is awaited, it means that the coroutine will wait until the Future is resolved in some other place.

**Asyncio Workflow:**

- **Define Coroutines**: Use `async def` to define functions that will act as coroutines. These can be thought of as non-blocking functions that may pause and resume their execution.
- **Create Event Loop**: Before running any coroutines, you need to get the event loop. In most cases, you'll use `asyncio.run()` which creates the event loop, runs the passed coroutine, and closes the loop.
- **Run Coroutines**: Use `asyncio.run()` to run the main coroutine and `await` to run other coroutines from within the main coroutine. Alternatively, use `loop.run_until_complete()` if you're managing the event loop manually.
- **Await Futures**: Use `await` to yield control and wait for the completion of an awaitable object (like coroutine or Future).

**Example of Asyncio in Action:**

```
import asyncio

async def main():
    print('Hello')
    await asyncio.sleep(1)
    print('World')

asyncio.run(main())
```

In this example, `asyncio.run(main())` starts running the `main()` coroutine and blocks until it's finished. Inside `main()`, `await asyncio.sleep(1)` simulates I/O by sleeping for 1 second. The above example may not work in Jupyter Notebook beca

**When to Use Asyncio:**

- Handling high-level structured network code.
- Implementing protocols using transports.
- Writing TCP/UDP/SSL clients and servers.
- Managing subprocesses.
- Distributing tasks via queues.

**Advantages of Asyncio:**

- Efficiently handles I/O-bound and high-level structured network code.
- Utilizes coroutines, providing an easier-to-use and more readable alternative to callbacks.
- Offers a significant performance improvement for I/O-bound tasks by enabling the use of asynchronous programming patterns.

Here's an overview of event loops, tasks, and futures in `asyncio` with practical examples:

## Event Loop

The event loop is the central execution device provided by `asyncio`. It runs asynchronous tasks, manages their execution, and handles all the network and system events.

**Example of Event Loop:**

```
import asyncio

async def main():
    print('Hello')
    await asyncio.sleep(1)
    print('World')

# Run the coroutine, which implicitly manages the event loop
asyncio.run(main())
```

In this example, `asyncio.run()` is a high-level function that runs the main function, which is a coroutine. It takes care of managing the event loop, which includes starting it, running the coroutine, and closing the loop after the coroutine completes.

## Tasks

Tasks are used to schedule coroutines concurrently. When you create a task, you schedule a coroutine to be run on the event loop.

**Example of Tasks:**

```
import asyncio

async def say_after(delay, what):
    await asyncio.sleep(delay)
```

```
    print(what)

async def main():
    task1 = asyncio.create_task(say_after(1, 'hello'))
    task2 = asyncio.create_task(say_after(2, 'world'))

    print(f"started at {time.strftime('%X')}")

    # Wait until both tasks are completed
    await task1
    await task2

    print(f"finished at {time.strftime('%X')}")

asyncio.run(main())
```

In this example, two tasks are created and scheduled to run concurrently. The `main()` coroutine waits for both tasks to complete before finishing.

## Futures

Futures are a low-level awaitable object that represents an eventual result of an asynchronous operation. You can await a future, which means that your coroutine will wait until the future is resolved somewhere else.

**Example of Futures:**

```
import asyncio

async def set_after(fut, delay, value):
    # Sleep for *delay* seconds.
    await asyncio.sleep(delay)
    # Set *value* as a result of *fut* Future.
    fut.set_result(value)

async def main():
    # Get the current event loop.
    loop = asyncio.get_running_loop()

    # Create a new Future object.
    fut = loop.create_future()

    # Run "set_after()" coroutine in a parallel task.
    # It will set a result for "fut" future.
    loop.create_task(set_after(fut, 1, '... world'))

    print('hello ...')
```

```
    # Wait for the result of the future object.
    result = await fut

    print(result)

asyncio.run(main())
```

In this example, a future object is created, and a task is scheduled to set the result of this future. The `main()` coroutine waits for the result of the future to be set before continuing.

Let's delve into some practical scenarios where `asyncio`'s event loops, tasks, and futures can be applied effectively.

## Scenario 1: Web Scraper

Imagine you're building a web scraper that needs to fetch data from multiple URLs simultaneously. Using `asyncio`, you can create an event loop to manage the tasks that handle the HTTP requests.

**Example:**

```
import asyncio
import aiohttp

async def fetch(session, url):
    async with session.get(url) as response:
        return await response.text()

async def main():
    urls = ['http://example.com', 'http://example.org',
'http://example.net']
    async with aiohttp.ClientSession() as session:
        tasks = [fetch(session, url) for url in urls]
        html_pages = await asyncio.gather(*tasks)
        # Process the HTML pages
        ...

asyncio.run(main())
```

In this scenario, `asyncio.gather` is used to run multiple coroutines concurrently and wait for all to finish, collecting their results.

## Scenario 2: Asynchronous API Calls

Suppose you need to make several API calls that don't depend on each other to complete. You can use `asyncio` tasks to perform these calls concurrently, thus saving time.

**Example:**

```
import asyncio

async def get_api_data(api_endpoint):
    # Simulate an API call with asyncio.sleep
    await asyncio.sleep(1)
    return f"Data from {api_endpoint}"

async def main():
    api_endpoints = ['/api/1', '/api/2', '/api/3']
    tasks = [asyncio.create_task(get_api_data(endpoint)) for
endpoint in api_endpoints]
    results = await asyncio.gather(*tasks)
    for result in results:
        print(result)

asyncio.run(main())
```

Here, `asyncio.create_task` is used to schedule the API calls, and `asyncio.gather` collects their results.

## Scenario 3: Database Queries

For applications that require executing multiple database queries that can run in parallel, `asyncio` can manage these queries as separate tasks.

**Example:**

```
import asyncio
import asyncpg

async def fetch_data(query, connection):
    return await connection.fetch(query)

async def main():
    conn = await asyncpg.connect(user='user',
password='password', database='db', host='127.0.0.1')
    queries = ['SELECT * FROM table1', 'SELECT * FROM
table2', 'SELECT * FROM table3']
    tasks = [fetch_data(query, conn) for query in queries]
```

```
    results = await asyncio.gather(*tasks)
    # Process query results
    await conn.close()

asyncio.run(main())
```

In this example, each query is run as a separate task, allowing for non-blocking database operations.

## Scenario 4: Handling Futures

Sometimes you may need to work with low-level futures, which can be awaited and used to retrieve results from asynchronous operations.

**Example:**

```
import asyncio

async def set_future_result(future, result):
    await asyncio.sleep(1)
    future.set_result(result)

async def main():
    # Create a Future object
    future = asyncio.Future()

    # Schedule the future to be set with a result
    asyncio.create_task(set_future_result(future, 'Future is
done!'))

    # Wait for the future result
    result = await future
    print(result)

asyncio.run(main())
```

In this scenario, the future's result is set by a separate task, and the main coroutine waits for this result.

# Data transformation

Data transformation is a crucial step in preparing data for analysis, and Python's built-in methods offer a wide range of functionalities for this purpose. Here are some common data transformation tasks and how you can accomplish them using Python's built-in capabilities:

## String Manipulation

Python provides a rich set of string methods that can be used to clean and transform text data.

**Example: Capitalizing the first letter of each word in a string.**

```
text = "hello world"
transformed_text = text.title()
print(transformed_text)
# Output: Hello World
```

## List Comprehensions

List comprehensions offer a concise way to create lists based on existing lists. They can be used for filtering and transforming data.

**Example: Squaring each number in a list if it's even.**

```
numbers = [1, 2, 3, 4, 5]
squared_evens = [x**2 for x in numbers if x % 2 == 0]
print(squared_evens)
# Output: [4, 16]
```

## Dictionary Operations

Dictionaries are key-value pairs and are useful for mapping operations.

**Example: Inverting a dictionary (swapping keys and values).**

```
my_dict = {'a': 1, 'b': 2, 'c': 3}
inverted_dict = {value: key for key, value in
my_dict.items()}
print(inverted_dict)
# Output: {1: 'a', 2: 'b', 3: 'c'}
```

## Set Operations

Sets are useful for removing duplicates and performing mathematical set operations.

**Example: Finding the unique elements in a list.**

```
my_list = [1, 2, 2, 3, 4, 4, 4]
unique_elements = set(my_list)
print(unique_elements)
# Output: {1, 2, 3, 4}
```

## Working with Tuples

Tuples are immutable sequences, typically used to store collections of heterogeneous data.

**Example: Swapping the values of two variables.**

```
a = 1
b = 2
a, b = b, a
print(a, b)
# Output: 2 1
```

## File I/O

Reading from and writing to files is often necessary for data transformation tasks.

**Example: Reading lines from a file and stripping newline characters.**

```
with open('file.txt', 'r') as file:
    lines = [line.strip() for line in file]
print(lines)
```

## Data Aggregation

Python's built-in functions like `sum`, `max`, `min`, and `len` can be used to perform simple aggregations.

**Example: Calculating the sum of numbers in a list.**

```
numbers = [1, 2, 3, 4, 5]
total = sum(numbers)
print(total)
# Output: 15
```

## Sorting

Python provides the `sorted()` function and the `.sort()` method to sort lists. You can sort by different criteria using the `key` parameter.

**Example: Sorting a list of tuples based on the second element.**

```
tuples_list = [(1, 'one'), (3, 'three'), (2, 'two')]
sorted_tuples = sorted(tuples_list, key=lambda x: x[1])
print(sorted_tuples)
# Output: [(1, 'one'), (3, 'three'), (2, 'two')]
```

## Filtering

The `filter()` function allows you to filter items out of an iterable.

**Example: Filtering out negative numbers from a list.**

```
numbers = [4, -1, 2, -5, 3]
positive_numbers = list(filter(lambda x: x > 0, numbers))
print(positive_numbers)
# Output: [4, 2, 3]
```

## Mapping

The `map()` function applies a function to every item of an iterable.

**Example: Converting all strings in a list to uppercase.**

```
strings = ['data', 'transformation', 'python']
uppercase_strings = list(map(str.upper, strings))
print(uppercase_strings)
# Output: ['DATA', 'TRANSFORMATION', 'PYTHON']
```

## Zipping

The `zip()` function is used to combine two or more iterables into a single iterable of tuples.

**Example: Combining two lists into a list of tuples.**

```
list1 = [1, 2, 3]
list2 = ['a', 'b', 'c']
zipped_list = list(zip(list1, list2))
print(zipped_list)
# Output: [(1, 'a'), (2, 'b'), (3, 'c')]
```

## Enumerating

The `enumerate()` function adds a counter to an iterable and returns it as an enumerate object.

**Example: Getting index-value pairs from a list.**

```
colors = ['red', 'green', 'blue']
indexed_colors = list(enumerate(colors))
print(indexed_colors)
# Output: [(0, 'red'), (1, 'green'), (2, 'blue')]
```

## Iterating with Comprehensions

You can use comprehensions with `dict`, `set`, and `tuple` to create new collections in a concise way.

**Example: Creating a dictionary with squares of numbers.**

```
numbers = [1, 2, 3, 4, 5]
squares_dict = {number: number**2 for number in numbers}
print(squares_dict)
# Output: {1: 1, 2: 4, 3: 9, 4: 16, 5: 25}
```

## Handling Missing Values

In real-world data, missing values are common and can be handled in various ways, such as removing the missing data or replacing it with a meaningful value.

**Example: Replacing missing values with the average of the list.**

```
data = [20, 22, None, 25, 24, None, 23]
average = sum(filter(None, data)) / len(list(filter(None,
data)))
cleaned_data = [x if x is not None else average for x in
data]
print(cleaned_data)
# Output: [20, 22, 22.8, 25, 24, 22.8, 23]
```

## Removing Duplicates

Duplicate data can skew analysis, so it's important to remove duplicates to ensure accuracy.

**Example: Removing duplicate entries from a list of records.**

```
records = [('Alice', 'Data Scientist'), ('Bob', 'Data
Analyst'), ('Alice', 'Data Scientist')]
unique_records = list(set(records))
print(unique_records)
# Output: [('Bob', 'Data Analyst'), ('Alice', 'Data
Scientist')]
```

## Standardizing Text Data

Text data often comes in various formats. Standardizing text to a common format is essential for consistent analysis.

**Example: Standardizing the case of strings in a list.**

```
names = ['ALICE', 'Bob', 'CHARLIE']
standardized_names = [name.capitalize() for name in names]
print(standardized_names)
# Output: ['Alice', 'Bob', 'Charlie']
```

## Parsing Dates

Dates can be represented in multiple formats, and standardizing them can be crucial for time series analysis.

**Example: Converting a list of date strings to a standard format.**

```
from datetime import datetime

date_strings = ['01-02-2020', '02/03/2020', '03-04-2020']
standard_dates = [datetime.strptime(date, '%d-%m-
%Y').strftime('%Y-%m-%d') if '-' in date else
datetime.strptime(date, '%d/%m/%Y').strftime('%Y-%m-%d') for
date in date_strings]
print(standard_dates)
# Output: ['2020-02-01', '2020-03-02', '2020-04-03']
```

## Cleaning Numerical Data

Numerical data can come with formatting issues like commas in numbers, currency symbols, etc.

**Example: Removing commas from strings representing numbers and converting to integers.**

```
price_strings = ['$1,000', '$2,500', '$3,300']
cleaned_prices = [int(price.replace('$', '').replace(',',
'')) for price in price_strings]
```

```
print(cleaned_prices)
# Output: [1000, 2500, 3300]
```

## Trimming Whitespace

Extra whitespace can cause issues when matching text strings.

**Example: Trimming leading and trailing whitespace from strings.**

```
dirty_strings = ['  Alice  ', 'Bob ', ' Charlie']
cleaned_strings = [s.strip() for s in dirty_strings]
print(cleaned_strings)
# Output: ['Alice', 'Bob', 'Charlie']
```

## Validating and Correcting Data

Ensuring data adheres to a defined schema or set of rules is important for data integrity.

**Example: Ensuring all phone numbers follow a specific format.**

```
phone_numbers = ['123-456-7890', '1234567890', '(123) 456
7890']
formatted_numbers = [re.sub(r'(\d{3})[- )(]*(\d{3})[- )]*(\
d{4})', r'(\1) \2-\3', num) for num in phone_numbers]
print(formatted_numbers)
# Output: ['(123) 456-7890', '(123) 456-7890', '(123) 456-
7890']
```

## Regular Expressions for Complex Patterns

Regular expressions are incredibly powerful for pattern matching and can be used to identify and extract complex data patterns, validate formats, and perform sophisticated replacements.

**Example: Extracting hashtags from social media posts.**

```
import re

posts = ["#fun in the sun!", "What a beautiful day! #happy
#sunny", "#amazing #world"]
hashtags = [re.findall(r'#(\w+)', post) for post in posts]
print(hashtags)
# Output: [['fun'], ['happy', 'sunny'], ['amazing', 'world']]
```

## Data Type Conversions

Converting data types is a common task in data cleaning, ensuring that numerical operations and comparisons are possible.

**Example: Converting strings to integers where applicable.**

```
data = ['123', '456', 'abc', '789']
cleaned_data = [int(item) if item.isdigit() else item for
item in data]
print(cleaned_data)
# Output: [123, 456, 'abc', 789]
```

## Handling Time Series Data

Time series data often requires alignment, normalization, and filling of gaps.

**Example: Filling in missing dates in a time series.**

```
from datetime import datetime, timedelta

# Sample time series data with missing dates
time_series = {
    '2020-01-01': 100,
    '2020-01-03': 105,
    '2020-01-04': 110
}

# Fill in missing dates
start_date = datetime.strptime(min(time_series.keys()), '%Y-
%m-%d')
end_date = datetime.strptime(max(time_series.keys()), '%Y-%m-
%d')
filled_time_series = {
    (start_date + timedelta(days=i)).strftime('%Y-%m-%d'):
time_series.get(
        (start_date + timedelta(days=i)).strftime('%Y-%m-
%d'), None)
    for i in range((end_date - start_date).days + 1)
}

print(filled_time_series)
# Output: {'2020-01-01': 100, '2020-01-02': None, '2020-01-
03': 105, '2020-01-04': 110}
```

## Data Validation

Ensuring that data meets certain criteria before analysis is crucial to avoid errors and misinterpretations.

**Example: Validating and correcting a list of ZIP codes.**

```
# Sample ZIP codes
zip_codes = ['12345', '6789', '98765']

# Validate and correct ZIP codes
valid_zip_codes = [code if len(code) == 5 else '0'*(5-
len(code)) + code for code in zip_codes]
print(valid_zip_codes)
# Output: ['12345', '06789', '98765']
```

These examples demonstrate how Python's built-in methods can be effectively used to clean and transform data in preparation for analysis. Each scenario requires a different approach, and Python provides the flexibility to handle these with ease.

# Data cleaning with regrex

Regular expressions (regex) are sequences of characters that form a search pattern, primarily used for string matching and manipulation. Let's delve into some common regex patterns, their use cases, and practical examples with expected outputs in Python.

## Literal Characters

In regex, literal characters are used to find exact matches in a string. This means that if you're searching for a specific word or sequence of characters, you use the literal characters in your pattern.

For instance, if you want to find the word `'dog'` in a sentence, you would use the literal characters `d`, `o`, and `g` in that order in your regex pattern. Here's how you might do it in Python:

```
import re

pattern = r'dog'
text = 'My dog is named Bingo.'
match = re.search(pattern, text)
if match:
    print('Found:', match.group())  # Output: Found: dog
else:
    print('No match found.')
```

In this example, the `re.search()` function searches through the `text` for the pattern `r'dog'`. When it finds a match, it returns a match object. Using `match.group()`, we can retrieve the part of the string where there was a match.

Now, let's consider a case where we have a pattern with multiple literal characters:

```
pattern = r'rain'
text = 'The rain in Spain stays mainly in the plain rain.'
matches = re.findall(pattern, text)
print('Matches found:', len(matches))  # Output: Matches
found: 2
for match in matches:
    print('Match:', match)  # Output: Match: rain (twice)
```

Here, `re.findall()` is used to find all occurrences of the pattern `r'rain'` in the `text`. It returns a list of all matches, and we can see how many times the pattern was found and print each occurrence.

Literal characters are case-sensitive by default. If you want to perform a case-insensitive search, you can pass the `re.IGNORECASE` flag to the search function:

```
pattern = r'bingo'
text = 'Bingo was his name-o.'
match = re.search(pattern, text, re.IGNORECASE)
if match:
    print('Found:', match.group())  # Output: Found: Bingo
else:
    print('No match found.')
```

In this example, even though the pattern is in lowercase and the text has 'Bingo' with an uppercase 'B', the match is still found because of the `re.IGNORECASE` flag.

# Character Classes

Character classes are a fundamental concept in regex that allow you to match any one character from a specified set. This set is defined by placing characters inside square brackets `[]`. For instance, the pattern `[abc]` will match any string that contains either 'a', 'b', or 'c'.

## Matching Vowels

To match any vowel in a string, you can use the pattern `[aeiou]`. Here's how it works in Python:

```
import re

pattern = r'[aeiou]'
text = 'The quick brown fox jumps over the lazy dog.'
matches = re.findall(pattern, text)
print('Vowels:', matches)
# Output: Vowels: ['e', 'u', 'i', 'o', 'o', 'u', 'o', 'e',
'e', 'a', 'o']
```

## Matching a Range

You can also define a range of characters using a hyphen `-`. For example,

`[0-5]` will match any digit from 0 to 5.

```
pattern = r'[0-5]'
text = '123456789'
matches = re.findall(pattern, text)
print('Digits 0 to 5:', matches)
# Output: Digits 0 to 5: ['1', '2', '3', '4', '5']
```

## Negating Character Classes

If you want to match characters that are *not* in a set, you can use the caret ^ symbol at the beginning of the class. For example, `[^aeiou]` will match any character that is not a vowel.

```
pattern = r'[^aeiou]'
text = 'The quick brown fox.'
matches = re.findall(pattern, text)
print('Non-vowels:', matches)
# Output: Non-vowels: ['T', 'h', ' ', 'q', 'c', 'k', ' ',
'b', 'r', 'w', 'n', ' ', 'f', 'x', '.']
```

## Special Characters

Most special characters (like `.` or `*`) lose their special meaning inside character classes. So, `[.]` will match a literal period, not any character.

```
pattern = r'[.]'
text = 'End of sentence. Start of another.'
matches = re.findall(pattern, text)
print('Periods:', matches)
# Output: Periods: ['.', '.']
```

## Combining Sets

You can combine ranges and individual characters. The pattern `[A-Za-z]` matches any uppercase or lowercase letter.

```
pattern = r'[A-Za-z]'
text = 'Regex 101: A to Z.'
matches = re.findall(pattern, text)
print('Letters:', ''.join(matches))
# Output: Letters: RegexAtoZ
```

Character classes offer a versatile way to specify a set of characters you want to match within a string. They are particularly useful when you need to match one of several characters in a single position.

## Predefined Character Classes

Predefined character classes are shortcuts for commonly used character sets. They provide a convenient way to specify a pattern that matches a common category of characters, such as digits or whitespace.

### \d - Digit

The `\d` character class matches any digit, which is equivalent to `[0-9]`. Here's an example:

```
import re

pattern = r'\d'
text = 'Room 101 in 1984.'
matches = re.findall(pattern, text)
print('Digits:', matches)
# Output: Digits: ['1', '0', '1', '1', '9', '8', '4']
```

The `\d` class is not just for finding individual digits; it can be used to find sequences of numbers, such as years or phone numbers. For example:

```
import re

pattern = r'\d+'
text = 'Call me at 555-1234 or 555-5678.'
matches = re.findall(pattern, text)
print('Phone numbers found:', matches)
# Output: Phone numbers found: ['555', '1234', '555', '5678']
```

In this example, `\d+` matches one or more digits, allowing us to extract sequences of numbers that could represent phone numbers.

### \w - Word Character

The `\w` character class matches any word character, which includes letters, digits, and the underscore. It's equivalent to `[a-zA-Z0-9_]`.

```
pattern = r'\w'
text = 'Python_3.8'
matches = re.findall(pattern, text)
print('Word characters:', matches)
# Output: Word characters: ['P', 'y', 't', 'h', 'o', 'n',
```

```
'_', '3', '8']
```

The \w class can also be used to find whole words, since it matches letters, digits, and underscores. Here's how you might use it to find usernames in a string:

```
pattern = r'\w+'
text = 'Usernames: user1, user_2, user-three.'
matches = re.findall(pattern, text)
print('Usernames:', matches)
# Output: Usernames: ['Usernames', 'user1', 'user_2', 'user',
'three']
```

Notice that `user-three` is split into `user` and `three` because the hyphen is not a word character.

## \s - Whitespace

The \s character class matches any whitespace character, including spaces, tabs, and newlines.

```
pattern = r'\s'
text = 'Hello, World!\nNew line here.'
matches = re.findall(pattern, text)
print('Whitespace characters:', matches)
# Output: Whitespace characters: Whitespace characters: ['
', '\n', ' ', ' ']
```

The \s class is useful for splitting text based on whitespace, which can include spaces, tabs, and newlines. For instance:

```
pattern = r'\s+'
text = 'Words\tseparated\nby different whitespace.'
matches = re.split(pattern, text)
print('Words:', matches)
# Output: Words: ['Words', 'separated', 'by', 'different',
'whitespace.']
```

Here, \s+ is used with `re.split()` to split the text into words, using any amount of whitespace as the delimiter.

# Dot

In regex, the dot `.` is a special character that matches any single character except for the newline character. It's one of the most powerful and commonly used metacharacters because of its ability to match almost anything.

Here's an example of how the dot can be used in Python:

```
import re

pattern = r'f.x'
text = 'The quick brown fox jumps over the lazy dog.'
matches = re.findall(pattern, text)
print('Matches:', matches)
# Output: Matches: ['fox']
```

In this example, the pattern `f.x` matches any three-character sequence that begins with 'f' and ends with 'x'. As you can see, it found the word 'fox' in the text.

It's important to note that the dot will not match a newline character by default. If you want the dot to match every character including the newline, you can use the `re.DOTALL` flag in Python.

```
pattern = r'f.x'
text = 'The quick brown fo\nx jumps over the lazy dog.'
matches = re.findall(pattern, text, re.DOTALL)
print('Matches including newline:', matches)
# Output: Matches including newline: ['fox', 'f\nx']
```

With the `re.DOTALL` flag, the dot in the pattern `f.x` now matches the sequence 'f\nx' as well, where `\n` represents the newline character.

The dot is extremely useful when you need to match a character without specifying what that character might be.

Another powerful use of the dot is in conjunction with quantifiers. For example, `.*` will match any number of any characters (except newline), effectively capturing everything in a line.

```
pattern = r'A.*?Z'
text = 'Start A123Z End AXYZ.'
matches = re.findall(pattern, text)
print('Matches from A to Z:', matches)
```

```
# Output: Matches from A to Z: ['A123Z', 'AXYZ']
```

Here, `A.*?Z` matches any sequence that starts with 'A' and ends with 'Z', capturing 'A123Z' and 'AXYZ'.

However, the dot can sometimes match more than you intend. To demonstrate, let's say you want to match a simple HTML tag:

```
pattern = r'<.*>'
text = '<div>Hello</div><span>World</span>'
match = re.search(pattern, text)
print('Match:', match.group())
# Output: Match: <div>Hello</div><span>World</span>
```

You might expect to match individual tags like `<div>` and `<span>`, but the pattern `<.*>` is greedy and matches the longest possible string, resulting in the entire line being matched. To make the dot match as little as possible, you can use the non-greedy version `.*?`:

```
pattern = r'<.*?>'
matches = re.findall(pattern, text)
print('Non-greedy matches:', matches)
# Output: Non-greedy matches: ['<div>', '</div>', '<span>',
'</span>']
```

Now, the pattern `<.*?>` matches each tag individually, as you might expect.

The dot is a powerful tool in regex, but it's important to use it carefully, especially when dealing with patterns that can match large portions of text.

# Anchors

Anchors are special characters in regex that do not match any character, but instead match a position before, after, or between characters. They are used to assert whether a string matches a specified position.

### ^ - Caret

The caret ^ matches the start of a string. If you use `^hello`, it will match 'hello' only if it appears at the beginning of a string.

```
import re

pattern = r'^hello'
text = 'hello there'
```

```
match = re.search(pattern, text)
if match:
    print('Match at the start:', match.group())  # Output:
Match at the start: hello
```

The caret ^ is not only used to match the start of a string, but in multiline mode (enabled with `re.MULTILINE` or `re.M` in Python), it matches the start of each line.

```
import re

pattern = r'^\w+'
text = 'Start of line one\nStart of line two\nAnd another
line'
matches = re.findall(pattern, text, re.MULTILINE)
print('Line starts:', matches)
# Output: Line starts: ['Start', 'Start', 'And']
```

In this example, `^\w+` matches the first word of each line in the text.

## $ - Dollar

The dollar $ matches the end of a string. The pattern `world$` will match 'world' only if it appears at the end of a string.

```
pattern = r'world$'
text = 'hello world'
match = re.search(pattern, text)
if match:
    print('Match at the end:', match.group())  # Output:
Match at the end: world
```

Anchors are particularly useful when you want to ensure that a pattern matches an entire string from start to end, not just any part of it.

```
pattern = r'^\d{3}-\d{2}-\d{4}$'
text = '123-45-6789'
match = re.match(pattern, text)
if match:
    print('Valid format:', match.group())  # Output: Valid
format: 123-45-6789
else:
    print('Invalid format.')
```

In this example, `^\d{3}-\d{2}-\d{4}$` checks for a string that matches the format of a Social Security number, with exactly three digits, a hyphen, two digits, another hyphen, and four digits.

Similarly, the dollar $ can be used to match the end of each line in multiline mode.

```
pattern = r'\w+$'
text = 'Start of line one\nStart of line two\nAnd another line'
matches = re.findall(pattern, text, re.MULTILINE)
print('Line ends:', matches)
# Output: Line ends: ['one', 'two', 'line']
```

Here, `\w+$` matches the last word of each line in the text.

Anchors are a powerful tool in regex that help you control where in the string your regex should match.

### Word Boundary \b

Another useful anchor is the word boundary `\b`, which matches the position between a word character and a non-word character.

```
pattern = r'\bcat\b'
text = 'The cat scattered his food.'
matches = re.findall(pattern, text)
print('Whole word "cat":', matches)
# Output: Whole word "cat": ['cat']
```

The pattern `\bcat\b` ensures that only the standalone word 'cat' is matched, not 'cat' within 'scattered'.

## Quantifiers

Quantifiers in regex allow you to specify how many times a character, group, or character class must occur in the string for a match to be found.

### * - Asterisk

The asterisk `*` matches the preceding element zero or more times. For example, `bo*` will match 'b' followed by any number of 'o's (including none).

```
import re
```

```
pattern = r'bo*'
text = 'A ghost boooed at me and I bolted.'
matches = re.findall(pattern, text)
print('Matches:', matches)
# Output: Matches: ['boooo', 'bo']
```

The asterisk * is often used when the presence of a pattern is optional, but it can also occur multiple times. For example, to match any word ending with 'ing' regardless of the prefix:

```
import re

pattern = r'\w*ing'
text = 'I am singing while the choir is ringing the bells for
the meeting.'
matches = re.findall(pattern, text)
print('Matches:', matches)
# Output: Matches: ['singing', 'ringing', 'meeting']
```

Here, `\w*ing` matches words like 'singing', 'ringing', and 'meeting', where the prefix can be of any length, including zero.

## + - Plus

The plus + matches the preceding element one or more times. Unlike the asterisk, the plus requires at least one occurrence for a match.

```
pattern = r'boo+'
text = 'A ghost booooed at me and I bolted.'
matches = re.findall(pattern, text)
print('Matches:', matches)
# Output: Matches: ['boooo']
```

The plus + is useful when you expect at least one occurrence of a pattern. For instance, to find sequences of consecutive digits:

```
pattern = r'\d+'
text = 'The year 2024 will mark the event.'
matches = re.findall(pattern, text)
print('Number sequences:', matches)
# Output: Number sequences: ['2024']
```

The pattern `\d+` finds one or more digits in a row, capturing '2024' in this case.

## ? - Question Mark

The question mark ? matches the preceding element zero or one time. It's used to indicate that the preceding element is optional.

```
pattern = r'bo?'
text='A ghost booooed at me and I bolted barely.'
matches = re.findall(pattern, text)
print('Matches:', matches)
# Output: Matches: ['bo', 'bo', 'b']
```

The question mark ? can be used to match patterns that may or may not be present. For example, to match the American and British spellings of a word:

```
pattern = r'colou?r'
text = 'The color of the sky is a beautiful colour.'
matches = re.findall(pattern, text)
print('Matches:', matches)
# Output: Matches: ['color', 'colour']
```

The pattern `colou?r` matches both 'color' and 'colour', with the 'u' being optional.

## {n} - Exact Number

Curly braces with a single number inside `{n}` match exactly `n` occurrences of the preceding element.

```
pattern = r'bo{2}'
text='A ghost booooed at me and I bolted'
matches = re.findall(pattern, text)
print('Matches:', matches)
# Output: Matches: ['boo']
```

When you need to match a pattern a specific number of times, you can use `{n}`. For example, to validate a binary number of exactly 8 bits:

```
pattern = r'[01]{8}'
text = 'The binary values are 11001010 and 101.'
matches = re.findall(pattern, text)
print('8-bit binary numbers:', matches)
# Output: 8-bit binary numbers: ['11001010']
```

The pattern `[01]{8}` matches sequences of exactly eight characters, each of which can be '0' or '1'.

## `{n,}` - n or More

Curly braces with a number followed by a comma `{n,}` match `n` or more occurrences of the preceding element.

```
pattern = r'bo{2,}'
text='A ghost booooed at me and I bolted'
matches = re.findall(pattern, text)
print('Matches:', matches)
# Output: Matches: ['boooo']
```

To ensure a pattern appears at least a certain number of times, `{n,}` is used. For instance, to find words with at least 5 letters:

```
pattern = r'\b\w{5,}\b'
text = 'These are some words of varying lengths.'
matches = re.findall(pattern, text)
print('Words with 5 or more letters:', matches)
# Output: Words with 5 or more letters: ['These', 'words',
'varying', 'lengths']
```

The pattern `\b\w{5,}\b` matches whole words that are at least five characters long.

## `{n,m}` - Between n and m

Curly braces with two numbers separated by a comma `{n,m}` match between `n` and `m` occurrences of the preceding element.

```
pattern = r'bo{1,3}'
text='A ghost booooed at me and I bolted'
matches = re.findall(pattern, text)
print('Matches:', matches)
# Output: Matches: ['boooo', 'bo']
```

The `{n,m}` quantifier is perfect for matching a pattern that occurs within a specific range of times. For example, to match an IP address octet:

```
pattern = r'\b\d{1,3}\b'
text = 'The IP address is 192.168.1.1.'
matches = re.findall(pattern, text)
print('IP address octets:', matches)
# Output: IP address octets: ['192', '168', '1', '1']
```

The pattern `\b\d{1,3}\b` matches sequences of 1 to 3 digits, which correspond to the octets in an IP address.

Quantifiers can be applied to individual characters, groups, and character classes to create flexible and powerful regex patterns.

### Combining Anchors and Quantifiers

Anchors can be combined with quantifiers to match patterns at specific positions. For example, to match a string that starts with one or more digits followed by a dash:

```
pattern = r'^\d+-'
text = '123-abc'
match = re.search(pattern, text)
if match:
    print('Match at the start:', match.group())  # Output:
Match at the start: 123-
```

In this example, `^\d+-` matches a sequence of one or more digits at the start of the string, followed by a dash.

## Groups and Capturing

In regex, parentheses `()` are used to create groups. These groups can serve two main purposes: they can group multiple tokens together to apply quantifiers to the entire group, and they can create capture groups to extract information from strings.

### Grouping Multiple Tokens

When you want to apply a quantifier to more than one character, you can group them together using parentheses. For example:

```
import re

pattern = r'(ha)'
text = 'He laughed "hahaha" because it was funny.'
matches = re.findall(pattern, text)
print('Matches:', matches)
# Output: Matches: ['ha','ha', 'ha']
```

Here, `(ha)`matches one or more occurrences of the group 'ha', capturing 'ha' thrice in 'hahaha'.

## Capturing Groups

Capturing groups are used to extract a substring from the matched string. Each pair of parentheses in a regex pattern creates a capture group. For example:

```
pattern = r'(\d{3})-(\d{2})-(\d{4})'
text = 'My number is 123-45-6789.'
match = re.search(pattern, text)
if match:
    print('Area code:', match.group(1))  # Output: Area code:
123
    print('Exchange:', match.group(2))  # Output: Exchange:
45
    print('Subscriber number:', match.group(3))  # Output:
Subscriber number: 6789
```

In this example, `(\d{3})-(\d{2})-(\d{4})` captures three groups corresponding to different parts of a Social Security number.

## Non-Capturing Groups

Sometimes, you may want to use groups for organization or to apply quantifiers, but you don't want to capture them. In such cases, you can use non-capturing groups, which are denoted by `?:` at the start of the group. For example:

```
pattern = r'(?:ha)+'
text = 'hahaha'
match = re.search(pattern, text)
if match:
    print('Match:', match.group())  # Output: Match: hahaha
```

Here, `(?:ha)+` matches 'hahaha' as a whole, but it does not capture 'ha' individually.

## Capturing Groups for Extraction

Capturing groups are not only useful for extracting simple strings but also for extracting complex patterns and reusing them within the regex or in the replacement strings during substitutions.

For example, to extract the first name and last name from a full name:

```
pattern = r'(\w+)\s(\w+)'
text = 'Jane Doe'
```

```
match = re.search(pattern, text)
if match:
    print('First name:', match.group(1))  # Output: First
name: Jane
    print('Last name:', match.group(2))  # Output: Last name:
Doe
```

Here, `(\w+)\s(\w+)` captures two groups separated by whitespace, allowing us to individually access 'Jane' and 'Doe'.

## Nested Groups

Groups can be nested inside other groups, which allows for capturing parts of a pattern within a larger matched pattern. For instance:

```
pattern = r'((\w+)\s(\w+))'
text = 'Jane Doe'
match = re.search(pattern, text)
if match:
    print('Full name:', match.group(1))  # Output: Full name:
Jane Doe
    print('First name:', match.group(2))  # Output: First
name: Jane
    print('Last name:', match.group(3))  # Output: Last name:
Doe
```

In this example, the outer group captures the full name, while the inner groups capture the first and last names.

## Backreferences

Capturing groups can be referenced later in the pattern with backreferences. This is useful for matching repeated sequences. For example, to find duplicated words:

```
pattern = r'\b(\w+)\s+\1\b'
text = 'This is is a test test sentence.'
matches = re.findall(pattern, text)
print('Duplicated words:', matches)
# Output: Duplicated words: ['is', 'test']
```

The `\1` in the pattern refers to the content of the first capturing group, allowing us to match an immediate repeated word.

## Named Groups

For more complex regex patterns, you can use named groups for better readability. Named groups are declared with `(?P<name>...)` and referenced with `(?P=name)`.

```
pattern = r'(?P<first>\w+)\s+(?P<last>\w+)'
text = 'Jane Doe'
match = re.search(pattern, text)
if match:
    print('First name:', match.group('first'))  # Output:
First name: Jane
    print('Last name:', match.group('last'))  # Output: Last
name: Doe
```

Here, `(?P<first>\w+)` and `(?P<last>\w+)` are named groups that capture the first and last names, respectively.

## Conditional Groups

Regex also supports conditional statements using groups. This allows parts of the pattern to match only if a certain group matched.

```
pattern = r'(?:Mrs?\. )?(?P<name>\w+)(?(1) \w+)?'
text = 'Mr. John Doe'
match = re.search(pattern, text)
if match:
    print('Name:', match.group('name'))  # Output: Name: John
```

The `(?(1) \w+)?` part of the pattern matches another word only if the first non-capturing group `(?:Mrs?\. )` matched.

Groups are a powerful feature in regex that enhance the pattern matching capabilities, allowing for complex and precise searching and data extraction.

# Alternation

Alternation in regex is represented by the pipe symbol | and allows you to match one of several patterns. It's like the logical OR in programming languages. When you use alternation, the regex engine will try to match each alternative in the order they are provided.

Here's a simple example:

```
import re
```

```
pattern = r'cat|dog'
text = 'I have a cat and a dog.'
matches = re.findall(pattern, text)
print('Matches:', matches)
# Output: Matches: ['cat', 'dog']
```

In this example, `cat|dog` matches either 'cat' or 'dog' in the text.

Alternation can be used within groups to specify a part of the pattern that has multiple alternatives:

```
pattern = r'(green|blue|red) apple'
text = 'I have a green apple and a red apple.'
matches = re.findall(pattern, text)
print('Matches:', matches)
# Output: Matches: ['green', 'red']
```

Here, `(green|blue|red) apple` matches 'green apple' and 'red apple'.

You can also use alternation to match entire patterns:

```
pattern = r'apple|banana|cherry'
text = 'I like to eat apple, banana, and cherry.'
matches = re.findall(pattern, text)
print('Fruits:', matches)
# Output: Fruits: ['apple', 'banana', 'cherry']
```

In this case, `apple|banana|cherry` matches 'apple', 'banana', and 'cherry'.

Alternation can be used for more than just matching single words; it can be used to match different patterns, each of which could be complex on its own. For example, you can use alternation to match different formats of phone numbers:

```
import re

pattern = r'(\(\d{3}\) \d{3}-\d{4})|(\d{3}-\d{3}-\d{4})'
text = 'Call me at (123) 456-7890 or 123-456-7890.'
matches = re.findall(pattern, text)
print('Phone numbers:', [match[0] if match[0] else match[1]
for match in matches])
# Output: Phone numbers: ['(123) 456-7890', '123-456-7890']
```

In this example, the pattern `(\(\d{3}\) \d{3}-\d{4})|(\d{3}-\`

d{3}-\d{4}) matches phone numbers in two different formats: with and without parentheses around the area code.

## Alternation with Groups

You can also use alternation within groups to create complex patterns. For instance, if you want to match different variations of a date format:

```
pattern = r'(\d{2}/\d{2}/\d{4})|(\d{2}-\d{2}-\d{4})'
text = 'Today\'s date is 03/18/2024 or 03-18-2024.'
matches = re.findall(pattern, text)
print('Dates:', [match[0] if match[0] else match[1] for match
in matches])
# Output: Dates: ['03/18/2024', '03-18-2024']
```

Here, `(\d{2}/\d{2}/\d{4})|(\d{2}-\d{2}-\d{4})` matches dates in 'MM/DD/YYYY' or 'MM-DD-YYYY' formats.

## Alternation for Optional Patterns

Alternation can be used to make certain parts of a pattern optional. For example, to match a word with optional prefixes:

```
pattern = r'un?credible|in?credible'
text = 'The story was incredible and the feat was
uncredible.'
matches = re.findall(pattern, text)
print('Matches:', matches)
# Output: Matches: ['incredible', 'uncredible']
```

The pattern `r'un?credible|in?credible'` matches 'credible', 'incredible', or 'uncredible'.

## Prioritizing Alternatives

When using alternation, the regex engine will try to match each alternative in the order they are provided. If you have overlapping patterns, the first one in the alternation will take precedence:

```
pattern = r'hand|handy'
text = 'The handyman had a hand in the work.'
matches = re.findall(pattern, text)
print('Matches:', matches)
# Output: Matches: ['hand', 'hand']
```

Even though 'handy' is present in the text, the pattern `hand|handy` matches 'hand' first because it appears earlier in the alternation.

Alternation is a versatile tool in regex that allows you to match multiple possible patterns within a single regex expression. It's particularly useful when you have multiple valid patterns for the input you're processing.

# Escape Characters

In regex, escape characters are used to remove the special meaning from metacharacters, allowing you to match characters like `.`, *, ?, and others literally. The backslash \ is the escape character in regex.

## Escaping Metacharacters

To match a metacharacter as a literal character, you precede it with a backslash. For example, to match a period `.`:

```
import re

pattern = r'\.'
text = 'Find the period. And another one.'
matches = re.findall(pattern, text)
print('Periods found:', matches)
# Output: Periods found: ['.', '.']
```

Here, `\.` matches actual period characters in the text.

## Escaping Special Sequences

Sometimes you need to match characters that are used in special sequences like `\w` or `\d`. To match these as literals, you also use the backslash:

```
pattern = r'\\w'
text = 'Match \w in text.'
match = re.search(pattern, text)
if match:
    print('Match found:', match.group())  # Output: Match
found: \w
```

In this example, `\\w` matches the literal string `\w`.

## Using Raw Strings

In Python, it's recommended to use raw strings when dealing with regex patterns. Raw strings are prefixed with `r` and treat backslashes as literal characters. They make it easier to write patterns without having to double escape backslashes:

```
pattern = r'\\d'
text = 'Match \d in 123.'
match = re.search(pattern, text)
if match:
    print('Match found:', match.group())  # Output: Match
found: \d
```

Here, `r'\\d'` is a raw string that matches the literal `\d`.

## Escaping in Replacement Strings

When performing substitutions with `re.sub()`, you need to escape the backslash if you want to include it in the replacement string:

```
pattern = r'\d+'
replacement = r'\g<0>'
text = 'Replace 123 with a backslash.'
result = re.sub(pattern, replacement, text)
print('Result:', result)
# Output: Result: Replace \123 with a backslash.
```

The replacement string `\g<0>` includes a literal backslash followed by the entire match.

## Escaping Within Character Classes

Within character classes, only a few characters need to be escaped, such as `]`, `-`, and `^`. For example, to match a hyphen or a square bracket:

```
pattern = r'[\-\[\]]'
text = 'Find the hyphen- or the brackets[] in this sentence.'
matches = re.findall(pattern, text)
print('Special characters found:', matches)
# Output: Special characters found: ['-', '[', ']']
```

Here, `[\-\[\]]` matches a literal hyphen, open square bracket, or close square bracket.

## Escaping Special Characters in Sequences

When you want to match a sequence that includes both special characters and normal characters, you need to escape only the special ones. For example, to match a dollar amount:

```
pattern = r'\$\d+\.\d{2}'
text = 'The total cost is $123.45.'
match = re.search(pattern, text)
if match:
    print('Dollar amount found:', match.group())  # Output:
Dollar amount found: $123.45
```

The pattern `\$\d+\.\d{2}` matches a dollar sign, followed by one or more digits, a period, and exactly two digits, representing a monetary amount.

## Escaping Escape Characters

Sometimes you need to match the escape character itself. In regex, you use a double backslash `\\` to match a single backslash:

```
pattern = r'\\'
text = 'This is a backslash: \\'
match = re.search(pattern, text)
if match:
    print('Backslash found:', match.group())  # Output:
Backslash found: \
```

In this example, `\\` matches a single backslash in the text.

## Escaping in Various Contexts

The context in which you use an escape character can change its meaning. For instance, `\b` outside of a character class matches a word boundary, but inside a character class, it matches the backspace character:

```
pattern = r'[\b]'
text = 'A\bB'
match = re.search(pattern, text)
if match:
    print('Backspace found:', match.group())  # Output:
Backspace found:
```

Here, `[\b]` matches a backspace character in the text.

## Escaping Non-Special Characters

Escaping a non-special character typically doesn't change its meaning, but it's good practice to avoid unnecessary escapes, as they can make the regex less readable:

```
# Unnecessary escape
pattern = r'\A'
# Better without escape
pattern = r'A'
```

In the first pattern, `\A` unnecessarily escapes a non-special character, while the second pattern is clearer.

Escape characters are a fundamental part of regex syntax that enables precise matching of patterns, including those containing special characters. They are essential for creating robust and accurate regex expressions.

# re methods

## search

The `search` method is used to search for a match of a regex pattern anywhere in the string. If the pattern is found, a match object is returned, containing information about the match: where it starts and ends, the substring matched, and more.

Here's an example:

```
import re

# Define the string
text = "The rain in Spain"

# Define the regex pattern
pattern = 'ain'

# Use search to find the pattern
match = re.search(pattern, text)

# Check if the pattern was found
if match:
    print("Found:", match.group())
else:
    print("No match found.")

# Output
Found: ain
```

In this example, `search` finds the first occurrence of the pattern 'ain' in the string. It can also search for patterns with special sequences, set operations, and even conditions.

For example, consider you want to find dates in a string that follow a particular pattern, such as "dd/mm/yyyy". Here's how you could use search:

```
import re

# Define the string

text = "Today's date is 19/03/2024."
```

```
# Define the regex pattern for a date
date_pattern = r'\d{2}/\d{2}/\d{4}'

# Use search to find the pattern
date_match = re.search(date_pattern, text)

# Check if the pattern was found
if date_match:
    print("Date found:", date_match.group())
else:
    print("No date found.")

# Output
Date found: 19/03/2024
```

In this example, `\b` is a word boundary that ensures the pattern is separate from other text, `\d` matches any digit, and `{n}` specifies exactly `n` occurrences of the previous element.

The `search` method can also be used with groups to extract specific parts of the matched pattern. For instance, if you want to separate the day, month, and year:

```
# Define the regex pattern with groups for day, month, and
year
date_pattern_grouped = r'\b(\d{2})/(\d{2})/(\d{4})\b'

# Use search to find the pattern
date_match_grouped = re.search(date_pattern_grouped, text)

# Check if the pattern was found
if date_match_grouped:
    print("Day:", date_match_grouped.group(1))
    print("Month:", date_match_grouped.group(2))
    print("Year:", date_match_grouped.group(3))
else:
    print("No date found.")

# Output
Day: 19
Month: 03
Year: 2024
```

Here, each pair of parentheses creates a group, and you can access the content of each group with the `group()` method by passing the group's index.

These examples illustrate the versatility of the `search` method for different scenarios.

# match

The `match` method is used to check for a match of a regex pattern at the **beginning** of the string. Unlike `search`, which looks for a match anywhere in the string, `match` only returns a result if the pattern occurs at the start. This is often used in scenarios where the format of the string is known and strict compliance is required, such as parsing protocol messages, validating user input, or checking for the presence of a specific keyword or phrase at the start of a string.

Here's an example to illustrate `match`:

```
import re

# Define the string
text = "The rain in Spain"

# Define the regex pattern
pattern = 'The'

# Use match to find the pattern at the beginning of the text
match = re.match(pattern, text)

# Check if the pattern was found
if match:
    print("Match found:", match.group())
else:
    print("No match found at the beginning of the string.")

# Output
Match found: The
```

In this case, `match` finds 'The' because it's at the start of the string. If we used 'rain' as the pattern, `match` would not find it because 'rain' is not at the beginning of the string.

Now, let's consider a scenario where we want to validate if a string is formatted as an email address right from the start:

```
# Define the regex pattern for an email
```

```
email_pattern = r'^[a-zA-Z0-9._%+-]+@[a-zA-Z0-9.-]+\.[a-zA-Z]
{2,}$'

# Define a valid email string
email_text = "example@email.com"

# Use match to validate the email
email_match = re.match(email_pattern, email_text)

# Check if the pattern was found
if email_match:
    print("Valid email format.")
else:
    print("Invalid email format.")

# Output
Valid email format.
```

The ^ in the pattern ensures that the matching starts at the beginning of the string. The rest of the pattern describes the structure of a typical email address.

One of the key aspects of the `match` method is its ability to use groups and special sequences to extract and manipulate parts of the matched string. For example, you can use parentheses `()` to create groups within your regex pattern, which can then be accessed using the `group()` method on the match object.

Let's consider a more complex example where we have a string containing a date, and we want to verify that it starts with a date in the format "yyyy-mm-dd" and then extract the year, month, and day:

```
import re

# Define the string
text = "2024-03-19 is the date of the meeting."

# Define the regex pattern with groups for year, month, and
day
date_pattern = r'^(\d{4})-(\d{2})-(\d{2})'

# Use match to find the pattern at the beginning of the text
date_match = re.match(date_pattern, text)
```

```
# Check if the pattern was found
if date_match:
    print("Year:", date_match.group(1))
    print("Month:", date_match.group(2))
    print("Day:", date_match.group(3))
else:
    print("The string does not start with a valid date.")

# Output
Year: 2024
Month: 03
Day: 19
```

In this example, the ^ at the beginning of the pattern ensures that the matching process starts at the beginning of the string. The pattern `\\d{4}` matches exactly four digits, which we interpret as the year, and similarly for the month and day. Each part of the date is enclosed in parentheses to create separate groups, allowing us to extract each component individually.

Another important feature of the `match` method is the use of flags, which can modify the behavior of the matching process. For instance, the `re.IGNORECASE` (or `re.I`) flag can perform case-insensitive matching, and the `re.MULTILINE` (or `re.M`) flag can make the ^ and $ anchors match the start and end of each line, rather than the whole string.

Here's an example using flags:

```
# Define the regex pattern with the IGNORECASE flag
pattern_ignorecase = r'^(the)'
text = "The rain in Spain"

# Use match to find the pattern at the beginning of the text
with IGNORECASE
match_ignorecase = re.match(pattern_ignorecase, text, re.I)

# Check if the pattern was found
if match_ignorecase:
    print("Match found with IGNORECASE:",
match_ignorecase.group(1))
else:
    print("No match found with IGNORECASE.")

# Output
Match found with IGNORECASE: The
```

In this case, even though the string starts with "The" and the pattern is in lowercase, the re.I flag allows for a successful match.

# fullmatch

The `fullmatch` method in Python's `re` module is used to check if the entire string matches the regex pattern. Unlike `search` and `match`, `fullmatch` will only return a match object if the whole string is a match for the pattern.

Here's an example to demonstrate `fullmatch`:

```
import re

# Define the string
text = "123-456-7890"

# Define the regex pattern for a U.S. phone number
phone_pattern = r'\d{3}-\d{3}-\d{4}'

# Use fullmatch to check if the entire string is a phone
number
full_match = re.fullmatch(phone_pattern, text)

# Check if the pattern was found
if full_match:
    print("The string is a valid phone number.")
else:
    print("The string is not a valid phone number.")

# Output
The string is a valid phone number.
```

In this example, `fullmatch` verifies that the entire string conforms to the pattern of a U.S. phone number. If there were any additional characters before or after the phone number, `fullmatch` would not return a match.

Now, let's consider a scenario where we want to validate an entire string as a hexadecimal color code:

```
# Define the regex pattern for a hexadecimal color code
hex_color_pattern = r'^#(?:[0-9a-fA-F]{3}){1,2}$'

# Define a valid hexadecimal color code
hex_color_text = "#1a2b3c"
```

```
# Use fullmatch to validate the color code
hex_color_match = re.fullmatch(hex_color_pattern,
hex_color_text)

# Check if the pattern was found
if hex_color_match:
    print("Valid hexadecimal color code.")
else:
    print("Invalid hexadecimal color code.")

# Output
Valid hexadecimal color code.
```

The pattern `^#(?:[0-9a-fA-F]{3}){1,2}$` ensures that the string starts with a #, followed by either three or six hexadecimal characters, and that's the entire string.

If you're working with a list of strings where each string must be a valid hexadecimal color code, you would use `fullmatch` to validate each string. The regex pattern for a hexadecimal color code is typically `^#(?:[0-9a-fA-F]{3}){1,2}$`, which means the string must start with a #, followed by either three or six hexadecimal characters, and nothing more.

Here's how you can use `fullmatch` to validate a list of color codes:

```
import re

# List of color codes
color_codes = ["#1a2b3c", "#fff", "#123456", "123456",
"#1a2g3c"]

# Regex pattern for a hexadecimal color code
hex_color_pattern = r'^#(?:[0-9a-fA-F]{3}){1,2}$'

# Validate each color code
for code in color_codes:
    if re.fullmatch(hex_color_pattern, code):
        print(f"{code} is a valid hexadecimal color code.")
    else:
        print(f"{code} is not a valid hexadecimal color
code.")

# Output
#1a2b3c is a valid hexadecimal color code.
#fff is a valid hexadecimal color code.
```

```
#123456 is a valid hexadecimal color code.
123456 is not a valid hexadecimal color code.
#1a2g3c is not a valid hexadecimal color code.
```

In this script, `fullmatch` is used to check each string in the `color_codes` list against the `hex_color_pattern`. Only strings that match the entire pattern are considered valid.

Another important aspect of `fullmatch` is its ability to work with flags, which can alter the behavior of the matching process. For instance, the `re.IGNORECASE` (or `re.I`) flag allows for case-insensitive matching, which can be useful when the case of the input string should not affect the validation:

```
# Define a case-insensitive pattern for a word
word_pattern = r'hello'

# String to match
text = "Hello World!"

# Use fullmatch with the IGNORECASE flag
if re.fullmatch(word_pattern, text, re.I):
    print("The string matches the pattern, ignoring case.")
else:
    print("The string does not match the pattern.")

# Output
The string does not match the pattern.
```

In this example, even though the fullmatch method is used with the re.I flag, it doesn't find a match because fullmatch requires the entire string to match the pattern, and "Hello World!" has additional characters beyond "hello".

# split

The `split` method is used to split a string by the occurrences of a specified regex pattern. The method returns a list of strings that were separated by the pattern. This is particularly useful for parsing data or extracting useful information from a string.

Here's a basic example:

```
import re
```

```
# Define the string
text = "The rain in Spain falls mainly in the plain."

# Define the regex pattern to split the string by spaces
pattern = ' '

# Use split to separate the string by the pattern
split_text = re.split(pattern, text)

# Print the result
print(split_text)

# Output
['The', 'rain', 'in', 'Spain', 'falls', 'mainly', 'in',
'the', 'plain.']
```

In this example, we split the string at each space, resulting in a list of words.

Now, let's consider a more complex scenario where we have a string with various punctuation and we want to split the string into words, ignoring the punctuation:

```
# Define the regex pattern to split the string by non-word
characters
pattern_non_word = r'\W+'

# Use split to separate the string by the pattern
split_text_non_word = re.split(pattern_non_word, text)

# Print the result
print(split_text_non_word)

# Output
['The', 'rain', 'in', 'Spain', 'falls', 'mainly', 'in',
'the', 'plain']
```

In this example, `\W+` matches one or more non-word characters (like spaces, punctuation, etc.), which are used as delimiters to split the string.

The `split` method can also be used with a `maxsplit` argument, which specifies the maximum number of splits to do. The remainder of the string is returned as the last element of the list. Here's how you can use it:

```
# Use split with maxsplit
split_text_maxsplit = re.split(pattern_non_word, text,
maxsplit=3)
```

```
# Print the result
print(split_text_maxsplit)

# Output
['The', 'rain', 'in', 'Spain falls mainly in the plain.']
```

In this case, the string is split at the first three occurrences of the pattern, and the rest of the string is returned as the last element of the list.

If you use capturing parentheses in a pattern, the text of all groups in the pattern will also be returned as part of the resulting list. This can be useful when you want to retain the separators for further processing.

Here's an example using capturing groups:

```
import re

# Define the string
text = "The rain in Spain falls mainly in the plain."

# Define the regex pattern to split the string and capture
the separators
pattern_capture = r'( )'

# Use split to separate the string by the pattern and capture
the spaces
split_text_capture = re.split(pattern_capture, text)

# Print the result
print(split_text_capture)

# Output
['The', ' ', 'rain', ' ', 'in', ' ', 'Spain', ' ', 'falls', '
', 'mainly', ' ', 'in', ' ', 'the', ' ', 'plain.']
```

In this example, the spaces are captured and included in the resulting list.

You can split a string using multiple delimiters by combining them in a pattern using the pipe | symbol, which acts as an OR operator in regex. This is useful when your string contains different types of separators.

Here's an example:

```
# Define the string with multiple delimiters
text = "The rain; in Spain, falls-mainly in the plain."
```

```
# Define the regex pattern to split the string by commas,
semicolons, or dashes
pattern_multiple_delimiters = r'[;,-]'

# Use split to separate the string by the pattern
split_text_multiple = re.split(pattern_multiple_delimiters,
text)

# Print the result
print(split_text_multiple)

# Output
['The rain', ' in Spain', ' falls', 'mainly in the plain.']
```

In this example, the string is split at each occurrence of a comma, semicolon, or dash.

# findall

The `findall` method in Python's `re` module is used to find all non-overlapping matches of a regex pattern in a string. It returns a list of all matches found. If one or more groups are present in the pattern, `findall` will return a list of groups; this can be tuples if the pattern has more than one group.

Here's a simple example:

```
import re

# Define the string
text = "The rain in Spain falls mainly in the plain."

# Define the regex pattern to find all occurrences of 'ain'
pattern = 'ain'

# Use findall to find all occurrences of the pattern
all_matches = re.findall(pattern, text)

# Print the result
print(all_matches)

# Output
['ain', 'ain', 'ain','ain']
```

In this example, `findall` returns a list of all occurrences of 'ain' in the string.

Now, let's look at an example with groups:

```
# Define the regex pattern with groups for 'ai' and 'n'
pattern_groups = '(ai)(n)'

# Use findall to find all occurrences of the pattern with
groups
all_matches_groups = re.findall(pattern_groups, text)

# Print the result
print(all_matches_groups)

# Output
[('ai', 'n'), ('ai', 'n'), ('ai', 'n'), ('ai', 'n')]
```

In this case, `findall` returns a list of tuples, each containing the matched groups.

An advanced use of `findall` is to search for patterns within a certain context using lookaheads and lookbehinds, which are zero-width assertions that don't consume any characters in the string. For instance, to find all words that are followed by a specific word, you could use:

```
# Define the string
text = "The quick brown fox jumps over the lazy dog."

# Define the regex pattern to find words followed by 'fox'
pattern_followed_by_fox = r'\b\w+(?= fox)'

# Use findall to find words that are followed by 'fox'
words_before_fox = re.findall(pattern_followed_by_fox, text)

# Print the result
print(words_before_fox)

# Output
['brown']
```

In this example, `\b\w+(?= fox)` uses a positive lookahead `(?= fox)` to find a word boundary followed by one or more word characters that are immediately followed by 'fox'.

The `findall` method can also be used with flags to modify the behavior of the pattern matching. For example, the `re.IGNORECASE` flag can be used to perform case-insensitive matching:

```
# Use findall with the IGNORECASE flag
words_ignore_case = re.findall(pattern_followed_by_fox, text,
re.IGNORECASE)

# Print the result
print(words_ignore_case)

# Output
['brown']
```

Even if 'fox' were in a different case, like 'FOX' or 'Fox', the pattern would still match because of the `re.IGNORECASE` flag.

When using groups within the `findall` method, it's important to understand how nested groups and non-capturing groups work. Nested groups are captured from the innermost level outward, which can affect the output of `findall`. Non-capturing groups, on the other hand, allow you to group part of a regex pattern without capturing the matched text.

Here's an example with nested groups:

```
# Define the string
text = "The rain in Spain falls mainly in the plain."

# Define the regex pattern with nested groups
pattern_nested_groups = '(a(i)n)'

# Use findall to find all occurrences of the pattern with
nested groups
all_matches_nested = re.findall(pattern_nested_groups, text)

# Print the result
print(all_matches_nested)

# Output
[('ain', 'i'), ('ain', 'i'), ('ain', 'i'), ('ain', 'i')]
```

In this example, the inner group `(i)` is captured along with the outer group `(a(i)n)`, resulting in tuples with two elements.

To use non-capturing groups, you can use the `?:` syntax within the parentheses:

```
# Define the regex pattern with a non-capturing group
```

```
pattern_non_capturing = '(?:ai)n'

# Use findall to find all occurrences of the pattern with a
non-capturing group
all_matches_non_capturing = re.findall(pattern_non_capturing,
text)

# Print the result
print(all_matches_non_capturing)

# Output
['ain', 'ain', 'ain']
```

In this case, the `?:` indicates that the group `(?:ai)` should not be captured, so the output is a list of strings rather than tuples.

By default, `findall` does not return overlapping matches. However, you can find overlapping matches by using lookaheads, as they don't consume characters in the string.

For example, to find overlapping occurrences of 'ain' in the string:

```
# Define the regex pattern to find overlapping occurrences of
'ain'
pattern_overlapping = r'(?=(ain))'

# Use findall to find overlapping occurrences of the pattern
overlapping_matches = re.findall(pattern_overlapping, text)

# Print the result
print(overlapping_matches)

# Output
['ain', 'ain', 'ain', 'ain']
```

In this example, the lookahead `(?=(ain))` allows us to find overlapping matches of 'ain'.

# finditer

The `finditer` method in Python's `re` module is similar to `findall`, but instead of returning a list of strings, it returns an iterator yielding match objects over all non-overlapping matches. This is useful when you want more information about each match, such as its start and end positions, or when dealing with a large number of matches that might be memory-intensive to store all at once.

Here's an example:

```
import re

# Define the string
text = "The rain in Spain falls mainly in the plain."

# Define the regex pattern to find all occurrences of 'ain'
pattern = 'ain'

# Use finditer to find all occurrences of the pattern
iterator_matches = re.finditer(pattern, text)

# Iterate over the matches and print details
for match in iterator_matches:
    print(f"Match: {match.group()} at Position: {match.start()}")

# Output
Match: ain at Position: 5
Match: ain at Position: 14
Match: ain at Position: 25

Match: ain at Position: 40
```

In this example, `finditer` provides an iterator that we loop over, and for each match, we can access the matched string with `match.group()` and the start position with `match.start()`.

The `finditer` method is particularly useful when you need to perform additional processing on each match, as you have access to the match object with all its methods and attributes.

Here's a more detailed example using `finditer`:

```
import re

# Define the string
text = "The rain in Spain falls mainly in the plain."

# Define the regex pattern to find words that contain 'ain'
pattern = '\w*ain\w*'
```

```
# Use finditer to find all words that contain 'ain'
iterator_matches = re.finditer(pattern, text)

# Iterate over the matches and print details
for match in iterator_matches:
    print(f"Word: {match.group()} starts at {match.start()}
and ends at {match.end()}")

# Output
Word: rain starts at 4 and ends at 8
Word: Spain starts at 12 and ends at 17
Word: mainly starts at 24 and ends at 30
Word: plain starts at 38and ends at 43
```

In this example, the pattern `\w*ain\w*` is used to find all words that contain 'ain'.

The `finditer` method is especially useful when you need to perform additional operations on the matches, such as replacing or modifying the matched text. Since it provides match objects, you can easily use other regex methods like `match.expand()` to perform substitutions within the matched text.

Additionally, `finditer` is more memory-efficient than `findall` when dealing with a large number of matches because it generates matches on the fly rather than storing them all in a list.

# sub

The `sub` method in Python's `re` module is used to replace occurrences of a regex pattern in a string with a replacement string. It's a powerful tool for string manipulation, allowing you to make multiple replacements in a single pass.

Here's a basic example:

```
import re

# Define the string
text = "The rain in Spain falls mainly in the plain."

# Define the regex pattern to replace 'ain' with 'ane'
pattern = 'ain'

# Define the replacement string
```

```
replacement = 'ane'

# Use sub to replace all occurrences of the pattern
replaced_text = re.sub(pattern, replacement, text)

# Print the result
print(replaced_text)

# Output
The rane in Spane falls manely in the plane.
```

In this example, `sub` replaces all occurrences of 'ain' with 'ane'.

Now, let's look at an example where we want to remove all non-alphanumeric characters from a string:

```
# Define the regex pattern to match non-alphanumeric
characters
pattern_non_alphanumeric = r'\W+'

# Use sub to remove all non-alphanumeric characters
cleaned_text = re.sub(pattern_non_alphanumeric, '', text)

# Print the result
print(cleaned_text)

# Output
TheraininSpainfallsmainlyintheplain
```

In this case, `\W+` matches one or more non-word characters, and we replace them with an empty string, effectively removing them.

The `sub` method can also be used with a `count` argument, which specifies the maximum number of replacements to perform. Here's how you can use it:

```
# Use sub with count
replaced_text_count = re.sub(pattern, replacement, text,
count=2)

# Print the result
print(replaced_text_count)

# Output
The rane in Spane falls mainly in the plain.
```

In this example, only the first two occurrences of 'ain' are replaced with 'ane', thanks to the `count` parameter.

The `sub` method can be enhanced with functions as the replacement argument, providing a dynamic way to determine the replacement string for each match. This is useful when the replacement depends on the specifics of the match.

Here's an example using a function as the replacement:

```
import re

# Define the string
text = "The rain in Spain falls mainly in the plain."

# Define the regex pattern to find all occurrences of 'ain'
pattern = 'ain'

# Define a function to use as the replacement
def uppercase_replacement(match):
    # Return the matched string in uppercase
    return match.group().upper()

# Use sub with the function as the replacement
replaced_text_function = re.sub(pattern,
uppercase_replacement, text)

# Print the result
print(replaced_text_function)

# Output
The rAIN in SpAIN falls mAINly in the plAIN.
```

In this example, the function `uppercase_replacement` takes a match object and returns the matched string in uppercase. The `sub` method applies this function to each match, dynamically converting 'ain' to 'AIN'.

Another advanced feature of the `sub` method is the use of backreferences. Backreferences allow you to refer to groups captured earlier in the pattern and use them in the replacement string.

For instance, if you want to swap words in a string:

```
# Define the string
text = "bad good, good bad"
```

```
# Define the regex pattern with groups for 'bad' and 'good'
pattern_swap = r'(bad) (good)'

# Use sub with backreferences to swap the words
swapped_text = re.sub(pattern_swap, r'\2 \1', text)

# Print the result
print(swapped_text)

# Output
good bad, bad good
```

In this case, `\2` refers to the second captured group (which is 'good'), and `\1` refers to the first captured group (which is 'bad'). The `sub` method replaces each match with the groups swapped.

The `sub` method is a versatile tool for string manipulation, allowing for complex replacements and text transformations. It's widely used in data cleaning, text processing, and automation tasks.

# subn

The `subn` method is similar to the `sub` method but with a slight difference. While `sub` replaces all occurrences of a pattern with a given replacement and returns the new string, `subn` also does this but returns a tuple containing the new string and the number of substitutions made.

Here's an example to illustrate `subn`:

```
import re

# Define the string
text = "The rain in Spain falls mainly in the plain."

# Define the regex pattern to replace 'ain' with 'ane'
pattern = 'ain'

# Define the replacement string
replacement = 'ane'

# Use subn to replace all occurrences of the pattern
replaced_text, num_subs = re.subn(pattern, replacement, text)

# Print the result
print(f"New String: {replaced_text}")
```

```
print(f"Number of substitutions made: {num_subs}")

# Output
New String: The rane in Spane falls manely in the plane.
Number of substitutions made: 4
```

In this example, `subn` replaces all occurrences of 'ain' with 'ane' and also tells us that there were 4 substitutions made.

Similar to `sub`, `subn` can also use functions as the replacement argument. This allows for dynamic computation of the replacement string based on the match object. It's particularly useful when the replacement logic is complex and requires conditional processing.

Here's an example using a function with `subn`:

```
import re

# Define the string
text = "100 cats, 23 dogs, 3 rabbits"

# Define the regex pattern to find numbers
pattern_numbers = r'\d+'

# Define a function to increment numbers by 1
def increment_number(match):
    # Convert the matched string to an integer, increment it,
and return as a string
    return str(int(match.group()) + 1)

# Use subn with the function as the replacement
replaced_text, num_subs = re.subn(pattern_numbers,
increment_number, text)

# Print the result
print(f"New String: {replaced_text}")
print(f"Number of substitutions made: {num_subs}")

# Output
New String: 101 cats, 24 dogs, 4 rabbits
Number of substitutions made: 3
```

In this example, the function `increment_number` takes a match object, increments the matched number, and returns the incremented number as a string. The `subn` method applies this function to each match, and also tells us the number of substitutions made.

`subn` supports backreferences in the replacement string, which allows you to refer to groups captured in the pattern. This can be used to rearrange text, retain certain parts of the matched text, or create complex replacements.

For instance, to reverse the order of dates in a string:

```
# Define the string with dates
text = "Event A: 12/31/2024, Event B: 11/30/2024"

# Define the regex pattern with groups for month, day, and
year
pattern_dates = r'(\d{2})/(\d{2})/(\d{4})'

# Use subn with backreferences to reverse the date format
reversed_dates, num_subs = re.subn(pattern_dates, r'\3-\1-\
2', text)

# Print the result
print(f"New String: {reversed_dates}")
print(f"Number of substitutions made: {num_subs}")

# Output
New String: Event A: 2024-12-31, Event B: 2024-11-30
Number of substitutions made: 2
```

In this case, \3-\1-\2 uses backreferences to rearrange the date format from "mm/dd/yyyy" to "yyyy-mm-dd".

The `subn` method combines the functionality of `sub` with the ability to track the number of changes made, making it a valuable tool for tasks that require both string manipulation and change tracking.

## escape

The `escape` method in Python's `re` module is used to escape all special characters in a string. This is useful when you want to use a string as a regular expression, but the string may contain characters that would be interpreted as special regex operators.

Here's an example:

```
import re

# Define the string with potential regex special characters
```

```
text = "This is a [sample] string. (With *special*
characters?)"

# Use escape to escape all special characters
escaped_text = re.escape(text)

# Print the result
print(escaped_text)

# Output
This\\ is\\ a\\ \\[sample\\]\\ string\\.\\ \\(With\\ \\
*special\\*\\ characters\\?\\)
```

In this example, `escape` adds a backslash before each character that has a special meaning in regex, such as `[`, `]`, `(`, `)`, `*`, and `?`.

The `escape` method is a quick way to ensure that a string is treated literally in a regex operation, without the risk of any part of the string being interpreted as a regex pattern.

# Error Handling

In Python, errors are inevitable, but they can be managed with error handling. The most basic form of error handling is the `try` and `except` block. Here's how it works:

```
try:
    # Code you want to try to run
    result = 10 / 0
except ZeroDivisionError:
    # Code to run if there is a ZeroDivisionError
    print("You can't divide by zero!")
```

In this example, attempting to divide 10 by zero raises a `ZeroDivisionError`, and the code within the `except` block is executed, printing a message to the user.

When a Python program encounters an error, it's said to have raised an exception. Each exception is a small self-contained object that represents an error condition. When this condition occurs, Python creates an exception object. If you write code that handles the exception, the program will continue running. If not, the program will stop and Python will print out a traceback, an error message that includes the details of where the exception occurred.

**Exception Hierarchy:** Exceptions in Python are organized in a hierarchy of classes. At the top is the `BaseException` class. Most exceptions are derived from the `Exception` class, which is a subclass of `BaseException`.

Here's a simplified hierarchy for some common exceptions you might encounter:

- `BaseException`
    - `SystemExit`
    - `KeyboardInterrupt`
    - `GeneratorExit`
    - `Exception`

- `StopIteration`
- `ArithmeticError`
  - `ZeroDivisionError`
  - `OverflowError`
  - `FloatingPointError`
- `LookupError`
  - `IndexError`
  - `KeyError`
- … (etc)

**Catching Exceptions:** You can catch different types of exceptions by specifying their names after `except`, and you can catch multiple types by using a tuple.

```
try:
    # Code that might raise an exception
    ...
except (TypeError, ValueError) as e:
    # Code to handle multiple exceptions
    print(f"An error occurred: {e}")
```

**The `else` Block:** You can also use an `else` block after your `except` blocks. The code inside the `else` block will run only if the code inside the `try` block didn't raise any exceptions.

```
try:
    # Code that might raise an exception
    ...
except ZeroDivisionError:
    # Code to handle the exception
    ...
else:
    # Code that runs if no exceptions were raised
    ...
```

**The `finally` Block:** Lastly, a `finally` block can be used to define clean-up actions that must be executed under all circumstances.

```
try:
```

```
    # Code that might raise an exception
    ...
except ZeroDivisionError:
    # Code to handle the exception
    ...
finally:
    # Code that runs no matter what
    ...
```

## `try`, `except`, `else`, and `finally`

The `try`, `except`, `else`, and `finally` clauses in Python form a combination of statements for a robust error handling mechanism. Let's delve into each one of them:

`try` **Clause:** The `try` block is used to wrap the code that might generate an exception. It allows you to test a block of code for errors.

```
try:
    # Code that may cause an exception
    result = 10 / 0
except ZeroDivisionError:
    # Code to handle the exception
    print("Handled ZeroDivisionError.")
```

`except` **Clause:** The `except` block lets you handle the error. You can specify different types of exceptions to catch them specifically. If you don't specify the exception type, it will catch all exceptions, which is not considered a good practice because it can make debugging harder.

```
try:
    # Code that may cause an exception
    ...
except ValueError:
    # Handle ValueError exception
    ...
except (TypeError, KeyError):
    # Handle multiple exceptions
    ...
except Exception as e:
    # Catch all other exceptions
    print(f"An unexpected error occurred: {e}")
```

`else` **Clause:** The `else` block is executed if no exceptions were raised in the `try` block. It's a good place to put code that should run only if the `try` block was successful.

```
try:
    # Code that may cause an exception
    ...
except SomeException:
    # Handle the exception
    ...
else:
    # Code to execute if the try block does not raise an
exception
    print("No exceptions were raised.")
```

`finally` **Clause:** The `finally` block is executed no matter what, and is typically used to perform clean-up actions, such as closing files or releasing resources, regardless of whether an exception occurred.

```
try:
    # Code that may cause an exception
    ...
except SomeException:
    # Handle the exception
    ...
finally:
    # This code will run no matter what
    print("This will always be executed.")
```

**Best Practices:**

- Use `except` blocks for known error types that you can handle.
- Avoid using bare `except:` clauses.
- Use `else` for code that should run only if the `try` block didn't raise an exception.
- Use `finally` for clean-up actions that must be executed under all circumstances.

These clauses provide a clear and manageable way to handle errors and ensure that your program can gracefully deal with unexpected situations.

# Custom Exception

Custom exceptions are a powerful feature in Python that allow you to create your own types of exceptions that can be raised and caught in your code. This can be particularly useful when you have specific error conditions that aren't adequately covered by Python's built-in exceptions.

Here's a detailed look into custom exceptions:

**Creating Custom Exceptions:** To create a custom exception, you define a new class that inherits from the built-in `Exception` class or from any other more specific exception class.

```
class MyCustomError(Exception):
    """Base class for other custom exceptions"""
    pass


class ValueTooLargeError(MyCustomError):
    """Raised when the entered value is too small"""
    def __init__(self, value, message="Value is too large"):
        self.value = value
        self.message = message
        super().__init__(self.message)

    def __str__(self):
        return f'{self.value} -> {self.message}'

class ValueTooSmallError(MyCustomError):
    """Raised when the entered value is too small"""
    def __init__(self, value, message="Value is too small"):
        self.value = value
        self.message = message
        super().__init__(self.message)

    def __str__(self):
        return f'{self.value} -> {self.message}'
```

In this example, ValueTooLargeError and ValueTooSmallError are custom exceptions that includes a constructor method (`__init__`) to initialize the exception with a specific value and message, and a `__str__` method to return a formatted string representation of the error.

**Using Custom Exceptions:** Once you have defined your custom exceptions, you can raise them in your code using the `raise` statement when a specific error condition occurs.

```
def check_value(value):
    if value < 10:
        raise ValueTooSmallError("The value is too small.")
    elif value > 100:
        raise ValueTooLargeError("The value is too large.")
    else:
        print("Value is within the proper range.")

try:
    check_value(5)
except ValueTooSmallError as e:
    print(e)
except ValueTooLargeError as e:
    print(e)
```

**Advantages of Custom Exceptions:**

- **Clarity:** Custom exceptions make your code more readable and self-documenting. When you raise a `ValueTooSmallError`, it's clear what kind of problem occurred.
- **Control:** They give you finer control over error handling. You can have different except blocks for different custom exceptions, which allows you to handle various error conditions differently.
- **Maintenance:** Custom exceptions make your code more maintainable. If the logic for an error condition changes, you only need to update the code in one place.

**Best Practices:**

- Naming: Custom exception names should be descriptive and follow the naming convention of ending with "Error".
- **Documentation:** Use docstrings to explain what each custom exception represents.
- **Inheritance:** Inherit from built-in exceptions to maintain compatibility with existing error handling.
- **Minimalism:** Don't create custom exceptions when built-in ones will suffice.

Custom exceptions are a key part of writing robust, clean, and well-organized Python code. They are especially useful in larger applications where you need to manage a lot of different error conditions.

# Assertion

In Python, an assertion is a sanity-check that you can turn on or turn off when you have finished testing the program. An expression is tested, and if the result comes up false, an exception is raised. Assertions are carried out through the use of the `assert` statement.

The `assert` statement has the following syntax:

```
assert expression, message
```

The `expression` is the condition that you assert to be `True` under normal circumstances, and the `message` is the error message that is displayed if the expression evaluates to `False`.

**When to Use Assertions:**

- To check for conditions that should never occur in your code.
- To make sure that assumptions about your program are as expected.
- To catch your own errors as early as possible in the development process.

**Example of Assertion:**

```
def calculate_average(grades):
    assert len(grades) != 0, "List of grades is empty."
    return sum(grades) / len(grades)

grades_list = []
average = calculate_average(grades_list)
```

In this example, if grades_list is empty, the assert statement will raise an AssertionError with the message "List of grades is empty."

**Handling Assertion Errors:** Assertion errors can be caught and handled like any other exception using the `try` and `except` blocks.

```
try:
    average = calculate_average(grades_list)
except AssertionError as error:
    print(error)
```

**Best Practices:**

- **Don't Overuse:** Assertions should not be overused. They are meant for situations where you are very confident that something should be true and want to verify it during development.
- **Not for Data Validation:** Assertions should not be used for validating data from external sources. Use regular checks and exceptions for that.
- **Disable for Production:** Assertions can be globally disabled with the `-O` (optimize) flag when running Python, so don't rely on them to perform critical checks in production.

**Caveats:**

- Assertions can be turned off globally in the Python interpreter with the `-O` and `-OO` flags, which can skip the evaluation of assertions and potentially lead to missing out on catching some bugs.

# Logging Errors

Python's `logging` module provides a flexible framework for emitting log messages from Python programs. It is part of the standard Python library and offers a lot of functionality that can be easily customized and extended.

**Basic Concepts of Logging:**

- **Loggers:** The objects that are used to log messages.
- **Handlers:** Determine what happens to each message logged to a logger.
- **Formatters:** Specify the layout of messages once a handler decides to emit a message.
- **Levels:** Indicate the severity of the messages being logged.

**Logging Levels**

Python defines a set of standard levels, in increasing order of severity:

- `DEBUG`: Detailed information, typically of interest only when diagnosing problems.
- `INFO`: Confirmation that things are working as expected.
- `WARNING`: An indication that something unexpected happened, or

indicative of some problem in the near future.

- `ERROR`: Due to a more serious problem, the software has not been able to perform some function.
- `CRITICAL`: A serious error, indicating that the program itself may be unable to continue running.

**Basic Logging Setup**

Here's a simple example of setting up logging in a Python script:

```
import logging

# Configure logging
logging.basicConfig(level=logging.INFO, filename='app.log',
filemode='w', format='%(name)s - %(levelname)s - %
(message)s')

# Log some messages
logging.info('This is an info message')
logging.error('This is an error message')
```

In this setup, we configure the logging to write messages with the level of INFO or higher to a file named `app.log`. We also specify the format of the log messages.

**Error Handling with Logging**

When an error occurs, you can use the logging module to log an error message:

```
try:
    # Code that might cause an error
    1 / 0
except ZeroDivisionError:
    logging.error('ZeroDivisionError: Attempted to divide by
zero')
```

For exceptions, you can use `logging.exception()` which logs an error message along with the traceback, providing more context about the error:

```
try:
    # Code that might cause an error
    1 / 0
except ZeroDivisionError:
    logging.exception('An exception occurred')
```

### Advanced Logging Configuration

For more complex applications, you might want to configure multiple handlers, set different logging levels for different parts of your application, or even create custom loggers.

The `logging` module is highly configurable, and you can set it up to log to files, send messages over the network, or even define your own handlers that do something completely different.

## Traceback

The `traceback` module in Python is a powerful tool for debugging, as it provides a standard interface to extract, format, and print stack traces of Python programs. When an error occurs, a traceback provides you with a report of the sequence of steps that the program took before it ran into the error.

### Printing the Most Recent Traceback

If an exception is caught, you can print the traceback using `traceback.print_exc()`. This function prints the traceback of the most recent exception caught in the `try` block:

```
import traceback

try:
    # Code that might cause an exception
    ...
except Exception:
    traceback.print_exc()
```

### Printing Stack Trace from an Exception Object

You can also print the traceback for an exception object by using `traceback.print_exception()`. This is useful when you have access to an exception object:

```
import traceback

try:
    # Code that might cause an exception
    ...
except Exception as e:
    traceback.print_exception(type(e), e, e.__traceback__)
```

### Getting Traceback as a String

Sometimes, you might want to get the traceback information as a string instead of printing it. You can use `traceback.format_exc()` to get the traceback as a string:

```
import traceback

try:
    # Code that might cause an exception
    ...
except Exception:
    tb_string = traceback.format_exc()
    print(tb_string)
```

### Inspecting the Traceback Object

Each exception has a `__traceback__` attribute, which is a traceback object. You can inspect this object to get detailed information about the stack trace:

```
import traceback

try:
    # Code that might cause an exception
    ...
except Exception as e:
    tb = e.__traceback__
    while tb is not None:
        print(f"File: {tb.tb_frame.f_code.co_filename}, Line:
{tb.tb_lineno}")
        tb = tb.tb_next
```

### Using Tracebacks in Logging

You can also integrate tracebacks with logging by using the `logging` module, which allows you to log exceptions along with the traceback information:

```
import logging
import traceback

try:
    # Code that might cause an exception
    ...
except Exception:
```

```
    logging.error("An exception occurred", exc_info=True)
```

Setting `exc_info` to `True` tells the logging module to add exception information and the traceback to the log message.